research for media production

media

MANUAL

MANUAL

second edition

research for media production

kathy chater

Focal Press
OXFORD   AUCKLAND   BOSTON   JOHANNESBURG   MELBOURNE   NEW DELHI

Focal Press
An imprint of Butterworth-Heinemann
Linacre House, Jordan Hill, Oxford OX2 8DP
225 Wildwood Avenue, Woburn, MA 01801-2041
A division of Reed Educational and Professional Publishing Ltd

Ⓡ A member of the Reed Elsevier plc group

First published as *Production Research: An Introduction*, 1998
Second edition 2002

British Library Cataloguing in Publication Data
Chater, Kathy
  Research for media production. – 2nd ed. – (Media manual)
  1. Television – Production and direction   2. Television
  programmes – Research
  I. Title   II Production research

Library of Congress Cataloging in Publication Data
A catalogue record for this book is available from the Library of Congress

ISBN 0 240 51648 6

For information on all Focal Press publications visit our website at:
www.focalpress.com

Typesetting by Florence Production Ltd, Stoodleigh, Devon
Printed and bound in Great Britain by Biddles Ltd, www.biddles.co.uk

PLANT A
TREE

BTCV
British Trust for
Conservation Volunteers

FOR EVERY TITLE THAT WE PUBLISH, BUTTERWORTH-HEINEMANN
WILL PAY FOR BTCV TO PLANT AND CARE FOR A TREE.

Contents

Acknowledgements

Like all researchers, I have drawn heavily on the knowledge and expertise of others when putting together this manual. Thanks are due to the members of the Production Research Group who developed the Skillset National/ Scottish Vocational Qualification (N/SVQ) in Production Research, particularly Antoinette Graves, Stephen Kelly, Geoff Prout and Maurice Raine; to Ashe Hussein for suggesting a way to come up with ideas; to Alexandra Barnett for the Internet tips; to Jane Mercer for tips on archive footage research; to Seb Tyack for information about video formats; to David Hudson for help with the copyright section and to Gill Moore for advice on the law. I also used material from various trade organizations, such as FOCAL International (the Federation of Commercial Archive Libraries), the Moving Image Society-BKSTS; the MCPS (Mechanical Copyright Protection Society) and the RSPCA. Any errors, however, are mine.

Introduction

This manual was originally published as a book based on the knowledge required for the National/Scottish Vocational Qualification (N/SVQ) in Production Research intended for those already working in the media. In revising it for the Media Manual series, information has been added to help students and young people who hope to work in the industry.

There never has been a clear definition of the job of researcher and, as technology develops and becomes easier to use, the divisions between different occupational sectors are becoming more fluid. Many researchers will expect to direct and edit short sequences. Production/broadcast assistants and secretaries will also do research. The word 'researcher' is not used to refer to a specific job, but to describe whoever happens to be responsible for finding a particular element to be included in a production. Other books in this series provide more detail about different production skills that the researcher may also be required to have and they are listed in the further reading list on p. 138.

This manual concentrates on television production because it is the area that covers the full range of research skills used in the media. The skills required are transferable across other sectors of the audio-visual industries, to radio and even to print journalism. As adaptability and flexibility are primary attributes of those working in the media, readers will easily be able to see the connections with their own preferred sector.

Types of productions

There are five terrestrial television channels and with the growth in cable, satellite and digital programming there are an enormous number of potential programmes, not to mention the non-broadcast market for corporate, training and educational productions. There has been a similar growth of radio stations. Although most radio programmes are music based, there are a number of talk shows that require research. The new media sector, producing CD-ROMs and the content of Internet sites, has grown in the last few years and is now a major area of employment.

How to find and assess facts and opinions is the same for all media. What differs is how the information is presented. The same research could be used as the basis for radio and television programmes, a corporate video and print articles. As most people working in these media are self-employed and typically are employed for only two-thirds of the year, it is worth developing additional skills to be able to work in more than one area of the industry. News journalism is a special skill. However, there are thousands of specialist magazines, some aimed at a particular trade and others at people with hobbies and leisure interests. Freelance journalism is worth considering to fill in the unemployed third of the year. It is also a useful way to maximize the time and effort put into a piece of research for a different medium.

Both television and radio programmes can be targeted at increasingly small and specialist audiences. As well as catering to their specific interests, age, sex, educational, social and ethnic backgrounds, programme-makers need to understand what they want at different times of the day. The same people may watch or listen to daytime shows, early evening shows, peak time and late night programmes, but expect different things from them. A good piece of advice is to watch television and listen to the radio critically – not just letting it wash over you.

The audience would broadly distinguish between drama, music and factual programmes. People working in directing and in the technical areas of the television industry would probably make the division between multi-camera work, either live or pre-recorded in the studio or an outside broadcast (e.g. a sporting event) and single camera location shoots. Picture editors distinguish between productions shot on film (which are now almost always dramas) and those on video, although film editors are often cross-trained to use video as well.

There are no very clear divisions for researchers, but the major distinction is probably the type of audience – are they watching or listening to be informed or to be entertained? Researchers tend to gravitate towards factual programmes or to entertainment. Here, too, there are overlaps – for example, a popular science programme might use the format and techniques of a studio games show. Holiday programmes both inform and entertain.

Programme genres

Factual:

- news
- current affairs
- documentary
- arts
- education
- science
- natural history
- sport
- religion.

Light entertainment:

- chat/talk shows
- lifestyle/consumer/leisure
- game/quiz shows.

Drama:

- single plays
- series, such as soap operas, where there are the same characters
- serials, where a single story is told over a number of episodes.

Jargon:

- stripped – same time every day
- strand – different programmes on a theme, for example current affairs, science and arts
- genre – type of programme
- magazine – programmes with a number of short items on a subject
- ratings – the number of people watching a programme.

Types of production

Radio is technically less complicated, so people can work across a wider range of programmes. Here the division is mainly made between studio-based programmes and those where the programme-maker goes out with a portable tape recorder and edits the results together later.

Who does what

What always surprises people when they first come into contact with a production, either because they get a job there or because they are appearing on a programme, is the number of people involved and how interdependent their work is. Writers for print – either books or periodicals – can closet themselves with their word processors for much of their working time, but someone employed on a film or television programme has to work with and depend on the actions and skills of a number of people. Radio can be a more isolated occupation – a pre-recorded and edited documentary may be made by one person and a tape recorder, although live programmes require more staff. Here, however, fewer people are needed than in film or television because radio technology is simpler.

Job titles differ according to the type of production and the company. The newsreader, newscaster or anchorman/woman on a news programme plays the same role of linking items as the presenter of a magazine programme, the disc jockey on a radio programme, the host on a chat show or the quizmaster/mistress of a quiz show. Their function is the same, yet what they are called varies. In news programmes, for example, there are subtle distinctions between a reporter and a correspondent – reporters cover news stories generally, a correspondent has a particular area of expertise, for example education or the environment. The audience, however, simply sees or hears someone describing a situation.

There are hundreds of job titles. Do not think in terms of jobs, but in terms of what needs to be done. On some productions, for example, the researcher will be responsible for booking people, on others it may be the PA and in big companies, such as the BBC, there are contracts assistants. Also, as technology changes and becomes easier to operate, multi-skilling increases and new job titles which reflect this are used. It is very common to find people carrying out two functions – producer/director is probably the most common.

The following is a selection of the most common job titles.

Radio production
- Editor – in charge of a number of programmes in a strand.
- Producer – has overall charge of individual programmes; is responsible for what happens behind the microphone; and recruits staff, talent and resources.
- Broadcast assistant – does administration, timing and some basic research.

In the studio:

- Studio manager
- Sound operator.

Television/non-broadcast production

- Editor – in charge of a number of programmes in a strand.
- Producer – has overall in charge of individual programmes; is responsible for what happens behind the cameras; and recruits staff, talent and resources.
- Director – responsible for what happens in front of the camera.
- Production manager – responsible for money, resources and logistics.
- Researcher – finds what is in the programme.
- Production assistant – general administration, scheduling shoots and timing.
- Production co-ordinator/secretary.

Technical:

- Cameraman/woman
- Sound Recordist
- Picture Editor (film or VT) – puts pre-recorded material together
- Dubbing Mixer – balances recorded sound, adds extra sound, for example background music and FX (effects), such as running water or gunshots.

Studio personnel:

- in the gallery – director, production assistant, vision mixer and technical manager (responsible for co-ordinating the sound and vision technical operatives).
- on the floor – floor/stage manager (link between gallery and floor), assistant floor/stage manager (props, general smooth running), floor assistant (runs scripts, brings in guests), autocue operator and warm-up man/woman.

Art department:

- Designer – responsible for the overall look of the set
- Graphics Designer
- Make-up Artist
- Costume Manager and Assistants
- Props Buyer.

Who does what

The role of research

Media studies courses lay emphasis on audience research and, indeed, this is of great importance to management, especially those involved in scheduling programmes. However, those actually making the programme do not normally carry out audience research or test public interest in an idea or new format. Of course, production staff must have a clear idea of their audience, but they do not undertake these tasks, which are handed over to specialist companies.

Production research is the process of finding the elements from which a production is made up – primarily information and contributors, but also additional material such as archive footage, sound and still pictures. The work involved, whether it is checking questions for a quiz show, finding celebrities for a daytime magazine programme or getting archive material, varies according to the kind of programme. On many productions, researchers will also be expected to originate ideas for items. Although the researcher has, in status and salary terms, a comparatively lowly job, good research is the key to a good programme. It does not matter how beautifully the shots are framed or how clearly the sound recorded, if what is being seen and heard is mediocre, the end result is a mediocre programme. It is the researcher's job to find what is seen and heard.

As programmes become more targeted on small audiences, their budgets get smaller too. This means that research is rarely carried out by a dedicated specialist and instead is carried out by someone who is fulfilling another function as well. Producers or directors may do their own research, assisted by the production/broadcast assistant or the secretary. Some researchers, however, will be expected to schedule shoots and even direct interviews and simple sequences. With improvements in technology that make cameras smaller, lighter and easier to use has come the job of video journalist (VJ) who researches, shoots, directs, edits, writes and presents the whole piece.

Big productions will have a single researcher; others may have more than one, especially where specialist skills such as archive film research are involved. Programmes with a fast turnaround (e.g. daily programmes) will also have several researchers. In news and current affairs, journalists, reporters and correspondents will do research as well as write scripts and present pieces to camera.

Research does not end with the first day of recording. Although the greater and most important part of the work should be done by then, the process continues sometimes until after transmission. This applies in particular if a book tied to the production is to be published, or the programme is asking for contributions from the audience. Who does what depends according to the type and scale of the production and the number of people in the team.

Role of research

To find, assess and make available the content of a production. This might include any or all of the following:

- information – facts (e.g. statistics, dates and biographies) and opinions
- people – members of the public, celebrities, experts, representatives and spokespersons, contestants and audiences
- locations
- props – objects (e.g. aromatherapy oils) and prizes.
- archive footage – specific events and stock footage (e.g. an aeroplane taking off)
- still pictures – photographs, slides and paintings (including engravings)
- sound – music, sound effects and spoken word.

Knowledge, attributes and skills of the researcher

Media studies is one of the most popular courses in higher and further education. About one-third of new recruits taken on by employers have some kind of media qualification; but two-thirds do not. This is because employers generally need some specialist knowledge connected with the programme they are making. Three years of studying the media only makes you an expert on the media, which is not much use if you are working on a political programme or a series about Chinese art. Many people get their first research job because of a particular field of knowledge, such as a language that few other people can speak, or experience in a related field, such as journalism. Therefore, a postgraduate media qualification is more useful because it adds the skills of production to expertise in another area.

Academic ability is only proof of the ability to pass exams. Most employers take on graduates because they regard a degree as a guarantee of a certain level of intelligence. More important than qualifications, however, are personal attributes and skills.

Attributes

A lot of people want to work as researchers in the media because they have the erroneous idea that it is glamorous – all meeting celebrities at parties and jetting off to exotic locations. Most research work is frustrating and time-consuming. Only enthusiasm and a desire to get the programme made will carry you through.

As researchers do much of their work in isolation, they have to take a great deal of responsibility. They not only have to find and assess material, they have to deliver it on time and within budget. This requires initiative – producers hire researchers to solve problems. No production in the entire history of broadcasting has gone as smoothly as planned, so adapting to change and flexibility are valuable.

Personal qualities:

- enthusiasm
- politeness
- persistence
- interest
- curiosity
- persuasiveness
- flexibility
- initiative
- tact.

As a result of the popularity of US-style shows where guests expose the most extraordinary experiences, there are now agencies to provide these kinds of people. In Britain, *The Vanessa Show* brought these agencies into disrepute when it was revealed that a researcher on the programme had knowingly booked an actor to pretend to be a member of the public. Other companies have found people misrepresenting themselves in order to get on screen, such as the boyfriend and girlfriend who said they were father and daughter. A suspicious mind has become a necessary attribute of the researcher working with members of the public.

Skills

Whatever the job title, the process of research covers more than the skills of finding the raw material of a production. Working as part of a team, negotiating skills, ways of making suggestions, anticipating and solving problems and meeting deadlines all depend on knowing how a programme is put together (including how much it will cost) and what contribution each member of the production team makes. The implications of how it is to be used, the legal constraints involved and a host of other considerations also have to be taken into account. Each programme will present different problems to which different solutions must be found. The ability to think laterally is vital.

Communication skills

The researcher is the bridge between the production team on one side of the camera or microphone and the people providing the programme content on the other. This requires strong interpersonal skills of communication, co-operation and negotiation.

Good communication is not just about speaking, it is also about listening and picking up clues from body language. There is no point in speaking clearly, concisely and persuasively to someone who is not listening because they have something on their mind. Pick your moment.

Summarize the main point(s) of what you want to say at the beginning of the conversation, make it clear why you need to talk and how the person you are speaking to is concerned. This should focus their mind on what you have to say.

While talking, from time to time check that you have been understood. This can be by summarizing what you have been saying and seeking agreement or by reading the other person's body language. For example, a frown can indicate either disagreement or non-comprehension – find out which.

While listening, concentrate on what the other person is saying. If you do not understand or need further detail, ask.

When you are discussing with people what needs to be done, take note of:

■ facts – what is needed, what problems there are.
■ decisions – what is to be done, how problems are to be solved.
■ actions – what needs to be done now and whose responsibility it is to do it.

Team working

You need to know what other team members do and what their responsibilities on this particular production are. In a small, independent company, it may be the researcher's job to negotiate and issue contracts to contributors or to clear the rights to use archive material or these tasks may fall to the production assistant. In a large company, there may be a contracts assistant or even a whole department to deal with them. You have to know whose responsibility it is – do not assume these things happen.

Negotiating might be called the art of making the greatest number of people the least unhappy. For example, you may think that a contributor you have found is essential to the production, but the director or producer may disagree and might prefer someone else, someone you consider weaker. Techniques to get your view accepted include shouting, laying out your arguments patiently and logically, and nagging gently for weeks on end. The technique you choose depends on who you are dealing with and how convinced you are of the validity of your position.

Anticipate what effect actions will have – both the implications on your work and the implications of your actions on others' work. If a complicated graphics sequence is required, you need to have an idea of how long it will take to produce, which mainly comes from experience or simply asking. You also need to know what other work the graphics designer is doing in order to decide when you have to give the information needed and how to explain the requirements. You must be aware of deadlines and what can be achieved within them. If you have only enough time to put together the bare outline of a situation, you need to decide what is essential and what else can be added if time and resources permit.

Compromises always have to be made. Often it is a matter of expense, but it may be that what is envisaged is not technically possible. Reasons have to be explained tactfully. Often something genuinely is impossible, but the ability to analyse a problem and think laterally is useful here. Always try to offer an alternative rather than saying a flat 'can't do'.

Time management

Given unlimited time and resources, anyone can produce the perfect programme. Unfortunately, there is never enough of either. Managing time properly is essential to get the best possible result on air. Note deadlines and work back from them. This does not mean just the production's transmission or delivery date and time, but being aware of when facilities (e.g. editing and transfer) are booked so you can deliver material to be used for them on time. Expect the worst and always have plan B in mind. Prioritize work – what needs to be done in the next hour, by the end of the day, by the end of the week?

Networking

Researchers rarely need to be an expert in anything, although they may get their first jobs through specialist knowledge of a particular subject. What they need to be is an expert in finding experts. As well as a good contacts book (see pp. 38–39) you will need a network of people who can give you information and suggest individuals with skills that you can use. In return, you must be willing to offer them the same service.

The term 'networking' is usually used in relation to getting jobs and, in an industry where employment patterns are so fluid, a good network is essential. It's not simply a matter of handing out business cards but of being part of an infrastructure that makes life easier for all those involved. When meeting somebody new, the bad networker thinks 'What can this person offer me?' The good networker thinks, 'What can this person offer my network?', whether it's a job or some particular expertise that will benefit a production being made by someone else.

Formal networking organizations are a good source of meeting people with a common interest and finding out what is happening. Of course, it is often important to be cautious about revealing everything you are doing in order to prevent ideas being stolen but you should not become so secretive and protective of your own sources that you get a reputation for being unco-operative and obstructive. Remember that it's a two-way process: if people don't know what you are looking for, they won't be able to help you.

Good networkers are:

- well-informed about what is happening in their industry
- curious about what is happening in other industries
- willing to offer advice and useful contacts
- positive.

Knowledge, attributes and skills of the researcher

Production stages

Programmes have to be originated, developed, recorded, edited and transmitted or, in the case of non-broadcast productions, delivered to the client. Who comes up with the idea, who does the development, the recording and the editing, and what part each person plays in the transmission or delivery is again a matter of what kind of production it is and how its day-to-day schedule is organized.

Every production goes through the following stages, whether it is done in a few hours for a news bulletin or over a year for a special programme to celebrate an important event.

- Originating – coming up with the idea and doing enough research to establish its viability. This may be done by a producer, a director or a researcher.
- Selling the idea to someone – in the case of complete programmes, this is usually the producer's role, but on established programmes and strands, researchers may be expected to submit their ideas to an editor or producer. Alternatively, in the case of non-broadcast productions, a company might commission a production either for corporate marketing or training purposes.
- Developing the idea further – gathering information, selecting contributors, finding illustrative material (e.g. stills, archive footage or sound) and deciding how best to put these together. This is the central function of research and, as indicated earlier, may be done by almost any member of the production team, including production/ broadcast assistants and secretaries.
- Managing the production process – getting and spending money, keeping track of it, scheduling the stages of production. The producer, production/unit manager, production co-ordinator and production assistant are the people most involved here, but researchers may also be involved with negotiating fees and contracts for contributors and archive material as well as organizing and scheduling simple recordings.
- Recording – the number and nature of the people involved here will depend on whether the production is recorded in the studio or as an outside broadcast (OB), either live or for later transmission, or using a single camera on location. Director, production assistant, camera operator, camera assistant and sound recordist are the job titles used here. For multi-camera recordings, there will also be vision mixers, technical managers, floor/stage managers, assistant floor/stage managers, lighting directors and a host of other people handling the technical aspects. In these days of multi-skilling, it is also worth noting that some of the roles on a portable single camera (PSC) recording on location may double up. Directors might operate the camera or record the sound. There may be no production assistant and the researcher might carry out the function of listing the shots or this may be done later in the office from the rushes.
- Editing, including writing any commentary needed – this is usually done by the director and picture editor but researchers may supervise the simpler sequences. In news and current affairs, journalists write their own scripts. On training and promotional videos, a specialist writer may be employed.

- Dubbing – the process of balancing and adding any additional sound needed is carried out by a specialist, supervised by the director/production assistant/researcher, depending on the complexity of the work required.
- Transmitting the programme, or delivering it in the case of, for example, a training video which is not broadcast – a lot of documentation is involved in transmission which is usually done by the producer/director and production assistant.
- Publicizing the programme may involve the whole production team or may be carried out by a specialist department within the broadcasting organization for which it is made. Alternatively, the arrangement of the press launch and publicity generally may be handed over to a PR company.

Production stages

1 Idea
2 Commission
3 Research
4 Managing the production
5 Recording
6 Editing
7 Dubbing
8 Transmission/delivery to client
9 Publicizing the production

Originating ideas

The increase in the number of broadcasting channels and radio stations means an enormous quantity of ideas are needed, not only for whole programmes but also for individual items within magazine programmes. There is also a large market for training, promotional and corporate videos, most of which are commissioned, but organizations may be open to suggestions if a gap in the market can be identified.

Sources of ideas

Every production starts with an idea. Relatively few of them are totally original. Often it is a matter of taking something that has been done before but presenting it in a novel way to try to convince the audience that this is new, relevant and exciting. This applies in particular to news and current affairs programmes – finding yet another angle on a long-running political crisis or the plight of the homeless consumes many hours in production meetings. You also need to think about how many people will be affected and ask why several million people should care.

In documentary areas, light entertainment or children's programmes, the scope for coming up with a new idea is much wider. In theory, a programme or programme item could be made about anything. Good research comes from being alert to every possibility and from making contact with people who are likely to bring you stories.

It is impossible to keep track of every programme that is broadcast to find out whether a programme about the same idea has already been made. This is where the Internet can be very useful as there are sites that hold this kind of information for different countries.

Many ideas, especially in news and current affairs programme-making, come from an article in a newspaper or magazine, but there are other sources. Work done for other productions, for example, often leads on to another programme.

The starting point may be a conversation overheard on a bus or in a shop or from a notice delivered by the local council through the letterbox. Established programme strands and broadcasting companies receive press releases and calls from regular contacts. A letter from a viewer or a letter in the correspondence column of a newspaper might form the starting point.

Ideas also need a peg on which they can be hung – why should this particular idea be done now? With general, news-oriented programmes, it is not enough that an idea is interesting, it must be topical. Particular days, weeks and months dedicated to an issue or celebrating something may provide a peg. This usually means that the idea must be developed well in advance. There is no central planning of dates like this – it is up to each individual organization to decide when they want to hold their events and finding out about them beforehand can be difficult. There are companies that provide this information and many broadcasters subscribe to their services, so it is worth investigating if there is a special date coming up. Trade and specialist magazines might also mention them in their forthcoming news sections.

Other pegs that can be used include the publication of a book, report or survey and the anniversary of an event, which is an old favourite. Unless you can make a case that the event changed the world in some respect, the response will be 'So what?'

Ideas

Ideas can come from:

- printed material (books, newspapers, periodicals, press releases, etc.)
- conferences
- trade fairs
- experts and specialists, including journalists
- other personal contacts
- previous programmes, both radio and television.

Ask yourself:

- Has this been done before?
- Has this been done in this way before?
- Why is it worth doing?
- What is the Unique Selling Point (USP)?

The USP, namely what your programme has that makes it unique, might be:

- a person
- previously unknown information
- an event
- a location.

Developing ideas

There are several ways to develop basic ideas. You can think of any three subjects, such as religion, geography and drama, and find a common link. Why do people in different countries react so strongly to religious portrayals in films and theatre? You can also start with a subject, such as old age, and combine it with something you can get a degree in, for example anthropology. You then need to find another factor to focus the programme, for example women. The final question that the programme will explore is 'How are old women treated in different cultures?'

You can get other treatments for the same subject by adding the subject of English Literature and asking 'How are old people treated in books?' Or you could add architecture and ask 'How are buildings designed for the elderly?' In each case, you would need to add a third element, perhaps a particular author or place to which people like to retire, such as Florida.

The diagram opposite shows just a few of the possibilities.

Alternatively, you may just have a feeling that it would be interesting to do something on a particular subject. Instead of plumping instantly for the most obvious angle, take time to explore possibilities. Mind Maps, devised by Tony Buzan (*Mind Map Book*), show ways to do this. When you have explored them all, you may find yourself with a series of programmes, rather than just one.

Next, do some basic audience research (this is probably the only time that a researcher will get involved in this). Tell people about your idea and see whether it interests them. Go for as wide a range of people as you can, not just your friends, who are likely to share your interests and views. What questions do they ask which might give you an indication of areas to consider in greater depth?

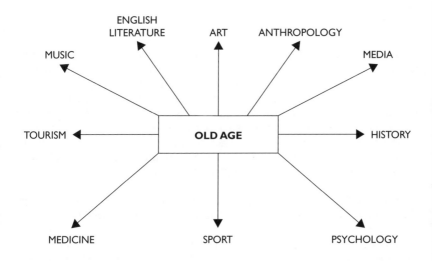

Treatments

So you have a good idea. It is not yet a programme or programme item worth watching. All ideas need to be translated from the medium in which they originated into what is called a treatment for a particular kind of production and audience. Many ideas are suitable for a choice of programmes so if one commissioner rejects it, you have alternative possibilities. It is a mistake to think that if one production is not interested in your programme idea, it is no good. What you must do, however, is present a fully developed treatment, not just the idea. People who commission productions are busy. You must do the work of translating the idea into possible programme and presenting it so they can understand what the audience will see or hear.

Those working regularly for a programme or company quickly learn the type of subject in which the editor or producer is interested. However, the treatment may have to be presented to an unknown person in order to get a commission. As well as doing enough preliminary research to establish that the production is worth doing, you will need to do some research on the people to whom it is being sold. Some broadcasters issue information about the kind of programme they are looking for and some hold meetings. You can always ring people who are likely to commission ideas and ask them what they want, but you also need to watch the kind of programmes they produce to decide if your idea is one likely to attract them and how it should be treated.

First, the medium for which the idea is being developed must be considered – whether it is to be for television, radio or non-broadcast productions (e.g. a training video). Things can be done on television that cannot be done on radio because they need to be seen. Conversely, it is very easy to make a television programme that is simply radio with pictures – the viewers miss nothing if they close their eyes while it is on.

If your idea is to be developed for a particular programme, you must think about:

- which channel it is broadcast on
- whether it is for a mass audience who know little about the subject or for a more specialized segment of the population who can be expected to bring more knowledge to it
- how old the majority of the viewers are likely to be
- what kind of social/educational/ethnic background it is aimed at
- what the programme format is – whether it is live or pre-recorded, studio based or recorded on location on portable single camera (PSC) or as an outside broadcast (OB); and whether a presenter/reporter is used.

The answers to these questions may limit what you can do. If you have no programme in mind at this stage, you must decide which would be the best way of presenting information to realize your idea.

Treatments

27

Methods of presentation

Further down the list of matters to be decided are the different ways of presenting the production's content. This starts with how the story is to be told, which may depend on the programme format. Is there to be an in-vision reporter or presenter? If not, are you going to have a commentary recorded by one of the professionals who do voice-overs or will you be using your subject's own voice? Perhaps the story would be best served by having no reporter or commentary at all, what is called 'fly-on-the-wall'.

In the visual media, remember to show, not tell. You might decide to reconstruct or dramatize events. This will usually mean hiring actors – very few people have the necessary skills to give the kind of performance needed, even if you are showing events that actually happened to them.

If you are going to use contributors (and the majority of programme do), how are they to be used? Will they be interviewed and if so how and where? A series of talking heads, perhaps interspersed with a few cutaway shots quickly becomes boring, so you will need to think of other ways to illustrate the story. Will there be some kind of performance or demonstration? If you are going to have a demonstration, who will give it – the presenter or a person with a special skill?

Will your production need illustrative material and if so what kind? Audio-visual productions may be enhanced by archive footage, but it might not be possible to find what you need, or it might be too expensive. What still pictures might you need either to supplement this or as an alternative? Facts and figures are best put across graphically.

Although pictures and graphics are, obviously, not relevant to radio, you need to think of how to use sound to create pictures in the listeners' minds. It can also add to the effect of audio-visual productions.

Non-broadcast productions, especially training videos, usually have a much higher level of dedication in their audience, so they usually have less demanding, and less expensive, methods of presentation.

Methods of presentation

Narrative methods:

- in-vision presenter/reporter
- out-of-vision commentary
- unscripted fly-on-the-wall
- dramatization/reconstruction.

Using contributors:

- talking heads
- group discussions
- phone-ins
- studio audience, who may take part in some way.

Visual methods of illustration:

- specially recorded film/video
- archive footage
- still pictures
- graphics/animation
- demonstrations using props and/or models.

Aural methods (which can be specially recorded or archive):

- music
- sound effects
- spoken word.

Selling the production

Once an idea has been worked out, the next stage is to sell it to someone. Whether you are doing this in writing or making a suggestion to the producer or editor at a production meeting, you need to summarize it in a sentence or two in a way that will grab your audience's attention and persuade them to watch it. What does this programme or item have that no other does? The short description in the programme listings published by magazines and newspapers is the kind of thing that is needed.

Next comes a longer description of the content of the production and how the various elements will be presented – specially shot footage, archive and interviews. Expand on the unique selling point (USP). Does the programme have access to a particular place or event, does it include people of particular interest, either because they are celebrities or because they have something of great interest to say? Does the programme contain information that radically changes the accepted view of a situation?

You have to anticipate likely problems, because they will probably be the first thing that the commissioner will ask you about. How much money will be available is always the major problem because it is never as much as you would like. The best idea in the world is useless to the programme if there is no money to do it. You must be aware of the cost of film crews, editing, special effects and graphics, not only in terms of money but also in time. If the programme is going out next week and the special effects you think essential will take 3 days to film and 5 days in post-production, you must forget it or think of a cheaper, faster way to achieve a similar effect. You do not always need to fly to India to do a programme about Indian customs. It may be something you could record in London or Leicester – less fun to do, admittedly, but you will have a better chance of realizing your idea.

Besides cost (always the commissioner's first consideration), you need to consider:

- what deadlines need to be met
- whether there are likely to be any logistical difficulties and, if so, what alternatives there are
- what copyright, legal and ethical considerations need to be taken into account.

Proposals

A proposal is a fully detailed and costed offer for a programme. As well as the treatment and budget, it will include the names of the key members of the production team. Commissioners, who often have a set format for proposals, are very interested in who will be working on the production. If they are handing over a large sum of money to make the programme and setting aside time in the schedule for broadcasting it, they want to be sure that it will be well-crafted and that it will come in on time and within budget.

Commissioners are not looking to reject proposals, but they will see the drawbacks, so you need to anticipate any possible problems. If they think you have not considered the obvious problems and how to solve them, they will not have confidence in your ability to deal with the unforeseen difficulties that always arise in the course of production.

Pitching a fully developed proposal to a commissioner is largely the responsibility of the producer and those involved in the management of the production rather than a researcher. However, the researcher may be involved in doing preliminary research for it and preparing the presentation.

- Is the meeting to be formal or informal?
- To whom is the presentation being made?
- What are their known interests?
- What is their level of knowledge?
- What are the key points that need to be conveyed?
- What benefits will the commissioner get from the production? This may not be simply audience figures as there might be some kind of prestige to be gained.

The basic ideas or treatment can be illustrated with selected press cuttings, stills and film clips. Formal presentations, usually to managerial level commissioners in the area of non-broadcast productions, will probably focus less on the content of the programme than on the audience and the cost. Press cuttings, stills and film clips can also be used, perhaps with the addition of overheads, slides and flip charts.

Starting the research

Once an idea or a proposal is accepted and the ways of realizing it are decided, the research goes ahead. If you did not originate the idea, but are the researcher on a production, you need to confirm what research will need to be done with the producer or editor. What is the aspect that is to be given most prominence and how will that be done? Who are the individuals or the kinds of people who will need to be contacted? Are there any potential problems?

The researcher must be able to assimilate very quickly the aims and nature of the programme being worked on, anticipate and assess the implications and discuss them tactfully with the other people involved in the production team.

It is easy to go away from a discussion with a very clear concept of the programme, only to find out after a considerable amount of work has been done that the producer saw it differently all along. Initially, you must ensure that everyone involved has the same view of how the story is to be developed. This may be done either in a production meeting with the rest of the team or one-to-one, but the process of clarification is the same in each case and depends on listening to what the other person is saying and ensuring that you are explaining yourself clearly. Summarize and feed back what you have understood: 'So you think we need to . . .?', 'So you feel this is a story about . . .?' and 'I see this as . . . is this right?' Some producers like everything to be very clear-cut from the beginning, but others may feel cornered and resent having to commit themselves early on. Some have firm ideas about how the story should be done, whereas others are open to suggestions.

Other aspects will have to be clarified with other members of the production team. There may be time already booked for doing any graphics or rostrum camera work, the recording days may already have been decided and you must know about them. This may affect which parts of your research you do first. Although ordinarily information and contributors would be sought first, if time to transfer archive film has been booked early on, efforts will need to be concentrated here initially. Whether this is done in writing or, as is much more common, verbally, you must summarize what has been agreed and note any constraints of time or money.

All these variables mean that researchers must be able to think quickly on their feet. No matter what has been planned, events can change either in response to technical problems or to a development in the programme treatment.

Keeping records

Research generates paper and before you start you need to organize a system to deal with it. A ring-binder or folder for each project will help. You might divide it into:

- contacts list
- typed up notes
- copies of material from newspapers, books, periodicals, leaflets, flyers, etc.
- correspondence
- paperwork connected with archive material and props
- shooting schedules, bookings for editing sessions, etc.

For your own notes, it is best to use a hard-bound book because single sheets of paper are easy to lose. Record the date of telephone conversations – it is sometimes important to know when they took place – and always get the names of the people to whom you talk. Print out copies of e-mails and faxes in case of computer problems.

Each source of information must be carefully recorded, especially if it is from a publication, which may have copyright implications or require acknowledgement. Note the title of the work, the author/s, the date and the publisher. If it is from a book, add the place of publication. Noting the page numbers will mean that you can go back to check if necessary. Documents, pictures, photographs or films from specialist libraries or archives will usually have a reference number, which should also be noted.

If information comes from interviews, there may be restrictions on its use – perhaps you have been told things off-the-record, or anonymity has been requested. If you have taped the interview, it should be clearly marked with the name of the interviewee and the date of the interview (see also pp. 56–7).

When you have finished a research project, go through the folder and note the names and numbers of useful contacts and sources. Put all the other papers together into a folder or file and store it somewhere in case of inquiries, which can come a surprisingly long time after transmission.

Methods of research

There are three stages of research. The first and cheapest is to speed read everything you can, either press cuttings or books, as background to the subject and perhaps get copies of programmes that have already been made about the same or a similar subject. You may find useful information and contacts in the programme files of previous productions made by your company.

From this, you decide which areas have not been covered or are worth following up in more detail. This can mean further, less superficial, reading, but at some point you will have to start talking to people, which involves more effort and expense, to narrow down which ones are likely to produce what you want.

This may be as far as the production research goes, especially if the programme has to be made and transmitted very quickly (e.g. news bulletins) or if the budget is small.

If you have more time, you should go out and experience the aspects that seem most promising – this can vary from simply meeting potential contributors and looking at locations to trying out activities. Which ones you decide to experience – religious cult meetings, training sessions or skydiving – and how far you go will depend on your own abilities and your sense of self-preservation.

Depending on the production, you may also want to commission a survey or questionnaire to find out what people do or think about a particular issue.

Stages of research

1 Read
2 Talk
3 Experience

Methods of research

- Read (printed matter or material from electronic retrieval)
- Watch/listen (audio and visual recordings)
- Talk (telephone or face-to-face)
- Experience (visits or try activities yourself)
- Commission surveys or questionnaires.

Speed-reading

Because the most efficient way of acquiring background information on a subject or situation is usually to read what has already been researched and written about it, you need to develop a technique that helps you to work through print fast, taking in the salient points.

When we read, we don't go from word to word along the lines. Our eyes fix on groups of words and also flicker up and down to the previous and next lines. We also tend to get bogged down on small groups of words. This slows us down and we don't necessarily get an overview of the whole text. It seems that the faster we read, the more we understand.

If you haven't already learned to speed read, you need to find the way that suits you best. There are various methods (the internet has several useful sites) but the following tips should help:

- Use something, like your hand, a card or a pen to guide your eyes down the page at a steady pace and to prevent re-reading.

- Most celebrity profiles in newspapers or magazines recycle the same basic facts, adding only one or two new pieces of information or insights so when using press cuttings to find out about a person, run your eye down the centre of the columns and when you see something that surprises or interests you, highlight it.

- If you are copying a lot of information from the internet, format it in two or three columns in 10pt type, so your eyes have less far to travel (this also reduces the amount of paper you use and have to file).

- Stories consist of exposition, development and resolution. If you're trying to read a novel at speed, either to interview the author or to make briefing notes, you can generally get the outline of the part that sets up the situation or plot (the exposition) from the jacket blurb or the press release so you don't need to read very much of the first part of the book. From previous works you will know if the author goes in for a lot of description, either of people or places so you will know how much weight to give to the paragraphs with such descriptions. The first sentence or two will give you the gist. When the action starts (the development) you need to read more and you should read the last part (the resolution) where all the plot strands are brought together fairly carefully – but don't give away what happens on air.

Sources of information

The company you work for may have a library or some arrangement with, for example, a source of press cuttings, without which no news-based programme can function efficiently. The main library in a city should also have the broadsheet newspapers on microfilm or CD-ROM or a regional newspaper will have archives that can be used for a local story. As well as these, you will find access to the following essential.

- A press guide, such as Willings, which lists all the newspapers, journals and trade magazines published in the UK and overseas. If you need to read articles in specialist journals or newspapers that are not available locally, you can use a national newspaper library, such as the British Library Newspaper Library.
- General directories of media contacts.
- Directories listing associations, societies and clubs. There are also publications covering charities, self-help groups, campaigns and pressure groups.
- Government publications, either printed or on CD-ROMs which contain official information and statistics on everything from the state of the economy to bed availability in hospitals.

These cover the whole country, but there are also regional publications covering a specific area. Some associations are now producing CD-ROMs of companies in their field and most industries produce a yearbook.

Most of these publications should be available in a large company but, if you work freelance, you should consider acquiring your own copies, so that you do not have to trek off to a library every time you need to look something up. Although reference books are very expensive if bought new, your local library may sell last year's copy as new editions come out. You could also check in charity shops. Finding last year's edition of a £90 yearbook for £9 is not only a good addition to your list of potential contacts, it is also tax-deductable if you are self-employed.

Sources of information

- National and local government.
- Quasi-autonomous non-governmental organizations (quangos), which are bodies funded by government to carry out a range of functions. The members of their boards are also appointed by government.
- Trade unions and professional associations, which are groups of people with a common interest created by what they do for a living.
- Clubs and societies which people belong to because they have a leisure interest in common.
- Charities, which can be divided into those run for a section of the population by people who are not affected by the issue the charity deals with and self-help groups which are run by those who have first-hand experience of a problem. The former tend to be larger and cover a wider range of activities, the latter smaller and focused on a specific area.
- Lobbying groups – trade associations, unions and charities may have a section that is devoted to lobbying for changes in the law as it affects their members. There are also single-issue organizations, which both monitor proposed legislation and make representations to government on general issues affecting all citizens, such as civil rights, censorship and electoral reform.
- Academic schools.
- Libraries and databases, including the Internet, largely gather information more indiscriminately than organizations that have a particular brief. There are general libraries and specialist ones that concentrate on a particular subject, such as women's history. Museums, too, are useful sources of information and experts on a particular subject. They also divide into the general and specialist.
- Individuals with a particular area of expertise who may not be attached to an organization; freelance journalists or those whose lifelong interest has made them experts in a particular field.

If you are pushed for time, as people usually are in news or current affairs, you can get a broad overview of a subject or situation by contacting the relevant government department, the trade association and a self-help or lobbying group, which will each give you their view. These will differ enough to give you a story and provide the 'balance' so precious to journalists and the broadcasting watchdogs.

Bear in mind that every area of human life has a newspaper or journal devoted to it. The journalists on these publications are very knowledgeable about their worlds.

Making a contacts book

The more sources you have access to, the more quickly you can find information. Your own contacts book is your most valuable asset. Addresses and phone numbers in it will come from programmes you have worked on and in certain areas of programme-making you will find yourself using the same ones over and over again. However, actively look for new people as audiences become bored when the same old Rent-A-Quote is trotted out each time a certain subject is raised.

You can increase your own list of contacts by collecting them in advance rather than waiting until you are working on a programme to start looking for them. If you keep a few index cards or a small notebook (which do not take up much room) about your person, you can quickly note any potentially useful organizations from, for example, newspaper articles or job advertisements. List the address, telephone number, fax and e-mail (if any) along with a brief note, if it is not obvious from the name of the organization, of what it does. If you are not on the Internet yourself, either at home or in the office, it is worth keeping a separate notebook of websites.

Newspapers or periodicals will often write about a self-help group that has just been set up to support and advise some section of the population or a club catering for unusual hobbies. They are among the most difficult to contact because they are usually started by one or two people operating from their front room. In time, they may grow to a national organization which will be listed in the telephone directory but, until then, are very hard to find in a hurry, yet can give very specific information and, equally important, contributors to a programme. The other problem with these small groups is that their organizers and addresses tend to change comparatively frequently.

While you are reading job advertisements, you can note useful organizations. A charity may be advertising for an administrator or secretary and, although you do not want the job, the organization may be of use some time in the future.

Trade fairs are also a good source of contacts and addresses as well as ideas. Established programmes are usually sent press releases and a press pass to them so, if you are feeling short of ideas and in need of some free hospitality, go along. It is more difficult for those outside a company to learn about these events, but they will be advertised in trade magazines. So if you work regularly in a particular field, such as science or music, look out for them in periodicals (which you should be reading anyway to keep up with your subject area).

Any change in the law will mean either the establishment of new groups to support or fight it or the abolition of organizations that are no longer relevant. Thus it is necessary to update your contacts book regularly. You also need to keep up with changes in personnel. It is not very professional to ring up asking to speak to someone who left the organization several years ago. An occasional call to people who have been helpful in the past or organizations which have been featured in your programmes will maintain contacts and should ensure they think first of you when a story comes up, but do not overdo this. They are busy people too.

Wherever you get your contacts from, you need to organize them in an easily accessible and logical way. Whether you keep index cards in a box, use a paper-based personal organizer or an electronic one, they should be grouped thematically rather than filed alphabetically. This is for three reasons:

- You won't always remember the exact name of an organization. Is it National Society of ... ; Royal Institute of ... or British Association of ...?
- Organizations change their names, either for image reasons or because they merge into larger groups.
- It wastes time to go through an alphabetical list picking out the ones dealing with a particular subject.

When you have the contacts dealing with a particular subject area grouped together, you can select it and all the different aspects come up so you have one list to work your way through. If, for example, you are doing something on vivisection, you will need to speak to both those who are for it and those who are against it, as well as people whose involvement in it is only peripheral but may have something unexpected or useful to contribute. Keeping all these together under a general title, like 'Animals', will give you a list that covers both the specific organizations you need and ideas for interesting sidelights. Of course many organizations will fall into two or three categories, so you must decide whether to duplicate the details or file them in the section most likely to be used.

While reading newspapers and periodicals, bear in mind the researcher's need to come up with ideas and either cut out items or note them on index cards. These can form a separate section in your filing system. As well as printed matter, you might also find it useful to record programmes, both television and radio, and it helps to keep a blank tape in the machine. This Ideas section can soon become overwhelming so will need regular weeding.

Sources of information

Using the Internet

If you or your company has access to the Internet, you will find that its resources are so vast that you can quickly get bogged down in the sheer amount of information available. The Internet should be used with caution, partly because of the potential to waste time and partly because there is usually no way of checking the accuracy or authority of the information on it. It can be difficult to tell whether a site with an official-sounding name is produced by a respectable organization, which has carefully researched the information on it, or a lone obsessive who is presenting his or her opinions as fact.

When you copy information, make sure you note the address and source, for example, a university. There are still copyright implications and you need to check the credentials of the site.

As well as being connected to the internet at the office or at home, you might think about getting an account with a service, like Hotmail, that can be accessed wherever you are, if you can't afford a laptop or handheld organizer with a modem. What you choose to put on it, whether it's your list of contacts for a current project or a shooting schedule, will vary according to what you are working on. You can also put your CV on it as you never know when your next job opportunity will arise.

10 tips for using the Internet

Note that 7, 8 and 9 are relevant to all methods of research.

1　Use a subject-based search, such as Yahoo if you know what topic you are after. Use a searcher, such as Infoseek when you can be specific. Try US search engines as well. Do not confine your search to just one. If you are looking for information on other countries, try their major search engines too (as long as you speak the language).

2　All search engines depend on you getting your keywords right. Take a moment with each of the engines to read the search tips which will tell you how to improve the chance of finding what you want.

3　If you are paying for your on-line time, spend a few minutes before you log on making a list of keywords. Have a strategy mapped out. Use the thesaurus in Word on your PC to find similar words and phrase. Do not forget that US search engines need US phrases and spellings.

4　Set yourself a time-limit. If after 10 minutes you have not found anything remotely resembling what you wanted, go for a walk (or log off if you are paying for the call) and think about it. Maybe you are using the wrong keyword. Maybe there is a better way to get to it, or a better engine to use. With time, you will become better at finding things quickly as you know what tools to use for the job.

5　Use the general search engines to find some good, well-linked pages on your topic and search the links on these pages as they are likely to be more relevant.

6　You can bookmark search results to return to at a later date.

7　Resist the urge to follow links that the search throws up that look interesting but are not particularly relevant. You have a specific objective when you search and you need to be disciplined.

8　Note down the source of your material, how credible the site is (is it an official site for that sort of information or not?) and the contact e-mail or number so you can check up on things.

9　Be info-aware when you look at sites. If it is not useful to you now, is it likely to be somewhere you want to note for the future? With experience, you will be able to judge these 'must remembers' fairly easily. They are often known as 'link sites' – a page where someone else has already collected together all the links to one topic.

10　If you can find out information faster by looking in a book or ringing a specialist, then do not use the Internet for the sake of it.

Collecting information

Once the organizations likely to give the information needed have been identified, they must be approached. This is usually done initially over the telephone so the first contact any person or organization has with a production is a telephone call. Their initial impression of the programme and its degree of professionalism will come from you, especially if you do not represent a long-established company or programme strand of which they have heard.

Anyone who is regularly asked for information over the phone becomes annoyed with people who do not know what they want because they have not bothered either to find out the parameters of the subject or to think about what they need to know. Thus, they are reluctant to help such people. They also dislike it when people ring up and want an enormous amount of information immediately. This is why it is important to read as much as you can before telephoning and to prepare what you want to say, writing down all the key points you need to cover. You may have interrupted a major crisis or rung at an inconvenient time, so check that the person can talk to you now or if you should arrange another time when he or she can concentrate on what you want to know.

Establish from the outset that you are working on a production and how the research is to be used. The extent of the help you require should be made clear and that will be the point at which any question of cost arises.

Databases usually make some charge and if you are accessing them through the Internet, the time you spend on-line will also cost. Other bodies may have restrictions on who they will give information to for free – usually a member of their association or a subscriber to their services. If you are going to need the organization to do some of the research for you, this must also be taken into account as they may want to charge for their time, depending on how much extra effort is involved.

However, there is a fine line to be drawn between establishing whether they will give their services free and putting ideas into their heads. Discuss whether and what kind of credit they could be given, but do not commit yourself. This is where researchers can come over all humble and unimportant – say that the final word must rest with the boss.

An adequate researcher will find out only what she or he is asked to do. An excellent researcher will find out what the producer did not know she or he wanted, and will actively look for the opposite point of view, for a range of sources that are likely to have different experiences or axes to grind. While selecting the sources you will contact (you could never hope to approach them all), you must decide which ones are the most authoritative, which ones represent the current view of a situation and which ones are fringe lunatics at the moment. Is your programme summarizing accepted wisdom or presenting a completely new theory?

Most of the information will suggest further avenues of research, but not all can be pursued. Decisions must be made about how much information each potential source is likely to yield, how vital such information will be, how long it is probably going to take and what it may cost. All these elements have to be balanced to produce the most effective result possible, which is not always the best that could be achieved given infinite time and resources. This is where you will have to discuss your findings and which avenues are to be further explored with the producer of the programme.

In the initial stages, record everything. Usually what is not said is of more interest than what is. Productions are usually made to add to what is already known, even if the production is summarizing the current situation. Think about the implications of the information and ask yourself 'Why is this?' Then use the possible answers to ask questions that will give a more complete picture of the subject being researched.

Dead ends

The initial stages of research are rather like a chain letter. You contact five people and each of them gives you some information and another three people to contact. Soon you will have more names and organizations than you can realistically talk to within your timescale, so you will constantly reassess which seem the most worthwhile avenues to pursue. However, there will come a point where one of your sources either cannot or will not help or suggest an alternative to contact.

You can go back and follow up some of the names you were given before and decided not to pursue. This often works but if it does not, lateral thinking is the solution. What related fields might provide the route back to your subject? Alternatively, the fact that you have hit a brick wall may mean that the programme is heading in the wrong direction and should be rethought. There may even be no story there. You may come up against a different brick wall if the story turns out to be too complicated to tell within the production's resources.

Verifying information

Note that this section does not refer to 'facts'. There are very few indisputable facts and a great number of people in academia and the media make a living out of contesting the accepted interpretation of events.

Broadly speaking, a fact is something that is capable of corroboration by external evidence. An opinion is an extrapolation from known facts. A commonly agreed 'fact' in the 90s was that the population of the UK was just over 58.25 million people. This figure was obtained through census returns. A research project, however, found evidence of under-recording in the UK's 1991 census taken at the time of an unpopular poll tax. How much under-recording is a matter of opinion. It was estimated to be about 1 million, but this cannot be proved. A fact is only a fact until someone comes up with a better alternative. Programmes can be made either by summarizing the accepted facts of a situation or disputing them.

When dealing with figures and tables, repeat the mantra 'Lies, damn lies and statistics'. Surveys very rarely publish the questions asked, yet these can be of vital importance. You can get people to agree with almost anything if you phrase it in the right way. There are questions that invite the answer

'Yes' and others that expect the answer to be 'No'. Surveys can also be constructed so that, after being guided through a series of questions, a person asking them would look a fool if he or she answered the last one in a particular way. Unscrupulous organizations (which can include the government) will publish the figures that relate to the last question without mentioning the careful way the preceding questions have been worded to get the answer they want.

Inevitably, this will result in contradictions and discrepancies. You can go back to your sources to look for other information or ask supplementary questions. Some may not be capable of resolution. Others can be resolved only by speculation. Be very clear about what is 'fact' and what is opinion – yours or anyone else's. Of course, the majority of people are not setting out deliberately to mislead or even lie. Some may be mistaken in what they say, so where there is a possibility of deception or error, tactful checking needs to be done.

If the brief has been well defined, you should not find it too difficult to decide what is relevant and what is not when you come to collect your research together. Knowing when to stop is always a problem. Researchers live with a nagging feeling that, given a little more time and money, they could find a single source of all information, rather than two sources and a gap; the perfect contributor rather than a choice between two who are very good; and the ideal location rather than one with a few drawbacks. Deadlines or the budget will impose a halt – at some stage you will have to say 'I can live with that.'

Inevitably, much of the material will turn out to be irrelevant to the programme brief. It helps to think of the brief in terms of a question to be answered. This should help to decide what is relevant and what is not. Does what has been found help to answer this question, or does it really apply to a different one? Extraneous material should be omitted from the final presentation, but not thrown away.

Often something that turns out to be irrelevant to the programme brief is in itself of such interest or importance that the brief may have to be re-evaluated, in which case you will have to discuss this with those who have the authority to make any changes.

Storing information

When you have gathered together and checked your research, the next step is to organize it before presenting your findings to the director/producer. This will help to clarify the story in your mind, especially if the research is taking place over a long period, and also to make sure that anything which initially seems irrelevant but might later prove important is not lost.

How you organize it will depend on the type of production. If it involves a large number of people, you will need to group them according to how important you think they will be. This is less of a problem for print journalists, but for television and radio, a lot can happen between first contact with a contributor and the recording. If someone drops out, you will have to find an alternative. If the production is thematic, for example, a programme about the causes of a war, then you will need to arrange your material by subject matter, which might be the political situation in both countries, religious factors, economics, etc. For a biographical profile, you might do it chronologically by year.

If you're putting your research information on computer, you need to think carefully about what you enter and who is allowed access to it. A balance must be struck between making your research available to the people who will need it – what will happen to all your carefully assembled material if you fall ill at a critical stage – and keeping sensitive material confidential. This is partly a matter of law (see pp. 130–4) and partly a matter of ethics. Even if it all remains in paper files, you should ensure that research material is securely stored, not just left lying around in the office.

Research tips

- Always carry a pen/pencil and notebook. You never know when you will hear something valuable or see a telephone number that will be useful.
- Pick up information leaflets from organizations you visit or local libraries in case they are useful for your current project or for one in the future.
- Before you start on a research project, make a list of the questions you know will need to be answered.
- Start off with organizations that are likely to be able to answer as many of these questions as possible and that are likely to know who can answer the questions they cannot.
- When you call an organization for information, consider whether they can also suggest potential interviewees. They might also know of locations where you can record and perhaps have archive footage or still pictures or even sound. This can save you a lot of your own research time and the production's money.
- Remember that there is always another point of view – ask yourself 'Where will I find it?'

Presenting research findings

At some stage, research findings must be presented to the producer or editor, either verbally or in writing. When you learn something exciting, it is a great temptation to tell the producer all about it straightaway. However, producers have many other things to think about. Equally, they do not want a blow-by-blow account of each problem as it arises. Of course, you have to let them know if there is a major difficulty, such as the non-availability of an important contributor, but in general, present your findings in well-considered sections to check that you are working along the right lines. This can be in a production meeting that the whole team attends or in an informal chat in the office. It is also a good opportunity to discuss in more detail how the information can be treated. As you gather information, bear in mind the different ways of putting it across, especially alternative courses of action that may solve problems.

The level of detail to be included will depend on the nature of the brief and on how much discussion you have already had with the other members of the team during the research process. On a long-term project, you may already have talked through most aspects, but on a programme with a very short timescale, you may have been entirely left to your own devices.

Whether you are doing it verbally or in writing, summarize the story and list the contributors and what they will say, highlighting their anecdotes or opinions and how well you think they will come across on screen. Then, depending on the other ways of presenting information which you have agreed, add details of locations, archive footage, graphics and stills which can be used for illustration along with any problems you can foresee.

Verbal presentations, especially if they are in a busy office, need care. Give a broad overview first, and then summarize at the end of each section giving opportunities to ask questions. If you've got visual aids, like photographs, use them – people remember what they've seen much better than what they've heard.

If you're writing notes, you still need to give an overview first. Use bullet points instead of continuous prose where possible. It's also a good idea to try to fit the information for each section, or subject area, on to a page, partly because people usually seem to read only the first page and partly because, if the second page becomes detached, important information may be lost. Alternatively you can number pages 1 of 1, 2 of 2, etc. (This is also a useful tip for your own notes).

Presenting research findings checklist

- What is the story?
- Who are the major contributors?
- What will each contributor do/say?
- Are there any dates when an important contributor will not be available?
- What illustrations will be needed, for example archive footage, still pictures, graphics or props?
- Where will the recording take place?
- Are there any restrictions on the location, such as dates or times?
- How much will it all cost?
- What alternatives can you suggest to solve problems?

Finding contributors

Factually based programmes, such as news and current affairs, consist largely of information and interviewees to illustrate the issue being raised. In documentary productions, the contributor(s) is likely to be the focal point. For a chat show, or an interview on a daytime magazine programme, the contributor is the whole point of the item.

Whatever the type of production, one of a researcher's major tasks is finding people to appear. While you are collecting information, you are almost always also looking for people to contribute directly to the programme by appearing on it. Contributors add authenticity and human interest. Although you may get a great deal of factual information from them, broadly speaking, they should appear on the programme for one of the following three reasons.

1 Authority – this is usually an expert on a subject or the spokesperson for an organization. However, people who fall into this category need not be academics or official figures. They can be experts because of their experiences or, and this is especially true of vox pops, general members of the public. Whatever their background, they will give opinions.

2 Experience – a person who has first-hand knowledge of a subject or an event. Such a person will relate anecdotes, or express emotion. People who are the subject of a portrait or appear on a chat show can be included in this group because it is their experiences that have made them of interest to the public.

3 Ability – someone with a skill to demonstrate. Quiz show contestants fall into this category.

News and current affairs or documentary programmes may need people to represent all three categories of interviewees. Indeed, a range of information, opinions and experiences should be represented whenever possible. News and current affairs usually have contributors from the first two categories (authority and experience), consisting of people who will offer contrasting opinions or experiences. If you are doing an item on the health service, for example, you might find a minister for the government's opinion on the situation, a representative from a professional association, such as the British Medical Association, who could either give their official opinion or their members' experiences, and a patient who would provide experience from a different perspective.

While gathering information for a programme, potential contributors must also be considered. They may come from all the sources listed on pp. 36–7 and indeed may be the people from whom the information comes. However, this is not always the case. Although information may come from a particular person in an organization, he or she might not be the right one to be interviewed for the programme. It might be more appropriate to use someone in a position of greater authority, who may need to be briefed by the informant before the recording is made.

Using the press

If you are trying to find people with specific experiences, you can advertise in the kinds of publications they are likely to read. Be specific about what you want. If you are too general, for example asking for people who have had a bad experience with divorce, hundreds will reply and you will waste a lot of time dealing with them all.

Never give your own home telephone number. This can be difficult if you are researching something on spec in order to do preliminary research before trying to sell the idea, but it is important to use an office number. People keep telephone numbers for years and you will get odd calls (some of them very odd) for a long time after the programme is made or you have moved on to another production. Again, this will waste time and there is the possibility that someone will trace your address and come round in person.

You can also use specialist magazines and local newspapers to obtain potential contributors by getting an article written about what you are doing. This method is particularly useful if you are trying to track down a specific person. It makes a good story, so the publication gets something of interest to its readers and, hopefully, you will get what you need as well.

Finding contributors

Selecting and using contributors

Keep the different methods of realization (see pp. 28–9) in mind when considering when and how to use contributors.

In factual programmes, contributors should not be used solely to present facts directly to camera. Visually, this is dull, although sometimes unavoidable in news programmes when there has not been enough time to set up alternative methods. Very rarely does the viewer need to see a contributor in order to understand factual information. Radio is a slightly different case, but even here facts can usually be put across more concisely in other ways. When you are selecting contributors who are going to be interviewed for the programme, look for the ones who have interesting opinions, concisely expressed, or good stories to tell. Those who can only give factual information may be helpful in giving you background material, but if they have nothing beyond this, they will not be able to add anything that will illuminate the facts, which is the major point of using contributors.

Figures are a case in point. When someone, usually a politician, starts reciting statistics, for example 'This government has increased spending by 3.5% in real terms and is now spending one and a half million pounds more than the previous government was 2 years ago . . .', the audience's eyes glaze and their fingers wander to the remote control. In a case like this, you do not really need the politician. You could use graphics, which put statistical points across much more economically and memorably. However, this is a studio technique as suddenly dropping a computer-generated pie chart into the middle of a sequence recorded on location looks bizarre.

On radio, facts can usually be better presented by the use of scripted material than by an interviewee. Presenting statistics on radio in an interesting way is notoriously difficult. Whenever possible, use fractions rather than numbers, for example instead of saying '63%' say 'just under two-thirds'.

If you have a presenter with a particularly abrasive style, you need to choose contributors who will not be thrown into stuttering confusion. In radio, particularly, the contributors should be chosen so their voices are distinguishable from each other, but this is also a good idea in television, which means seeking out not just different tonal qualities of voice, but also accents (which may also be an indication of social background).

Selecting contributors checklist

Do you need a contributor for:

- authority
- experience
- ability?

Is what you need from the contributor:

- opinion
- anecdote
- emotion
- demonstration?

Consider where you will find contributors to cover the range of:

- age
- educational background
- social background
- ethnic background
- degree and nature of any disability.

Is the contributor:

- knowledgeable
- articulate
- enthusiastic
- someone with whom the audience can identify?

The kinds of people needed for a programme will depend in part on the subject and in part on the targeted audience. The story and the contributors should complement each other. If your programme is discussing women's rights, the majority, if not all, of the contributors should be women. They should also come from a range of ages and backgrounds. Inevitably, you will look with more interest and approval on people who reflect aspects of your experience, but you should aim to reflect a spectrum of experiences.

Contacting contributors

Most of the time, you will contact potential contributors directly, but there are occasions when you will need to go through a third party. Celebrities, for example, should be contacted through their agents; representatives of government or large organizations through the press department of their ministry or company; and MPs through their political party. It is tempting to evade these gatekeepers and it may work once. However, you will then find that the agent or representative will be annoyed by your actions and be less than helpful in future.

If you are working in a sensitive personal area, it may be preferable to involve another person, someone the potential contributor already knows and trusts, to approach him or her on your behalf. The organizer of a self-help group from whom you obtained information about, for example, cot deaths will probably be able to suggest a member of the group who could be interviewed for the programme about his or her experience and to act as go-between.

Your first contact with a potential interviewee is usually by telephone. This allows you to do a preliminary assessment of their suitability. In radio what you hear is what you get, so the decision to record a contributor can be made on the telephone call alone. As audio tape is much cheaper than a full crew, interviews for radio are usually recorded at the first meeting so programme-makers do not need to do a preliminary, face-to-face research interview.

In television, there are times when the researcher may decide to go straight to a recording rather than conducting a research interview first. There are advantages to both options. A filmed interview will give the potential contributor time to think about what to say, but the freshness and immediacy of recording first thoughts may be lost. If the interviewee is essential to the programme, such as the spouse of a person about whom a biography or obituary is being made, it is probably unnecessary to do a full research interview first, although it will be essential to establish trust through a personal connection in advance.

If you are going to do a recording straightaway, you need to do much more planning and research before calling the potential interviewee, but you must still do some if you expect to do a research interview. Have a list of topics you need to cover and note them down in keyword form.

You learn a lot from the initial telephone call to potential contributors. Does the person sound confident, in charge and enthusiastic about the subject? Can they put across views clearly and simply? Are there any good stories they can tell? Do they have any communication problems, such as a very strong accent, a speech impediment or an irritating mannerism, such as saying 'Innit?' every few words? These need not preclude them from the programme – you might be doing something on speech impediments or inarticulacy – but they are factors to be taken into account.

Contacting contributors checklist

Before you call

- Do your research. Is this the right person? What do you need from them (keywords)? What is in it for them (known as WIIFT) – what they will get out of appearing?
- Think about the purpose of the interview. Is it to obtain facts, opinions, emotive personal testimony or stories about experiences?

When you call

- Check it is a good time to talk. If it is not, arrange a time to call back and do it.
- Explain what you want from them.
- Talk to them, using your list of keywords to make sure you cover all the points, but do not stick so rigidly to it that you don't follow up interesting sidelines.
- Use pauses to give people time to think (people rush to fill silences on the telephone and they may tell you something really interesting if you wait).
- Assess whether they are knowledgeable, enthusiastic and intelligible.
- Decide if they are the right person. If not, can they suggest someone else? (However, do not tell them that they are not suitable. Be tactful.)
- For television you will probably have to meet them for further assessment. Arrange a time and place, but do not promise them that they will be included.

Specialist contributor research

In light entertainment programmes, there are specialist researchers whose job is to obtain guests, either celebrities or contestants on quiz shows.

Celebrity research

Those who go into celebrity research usually have a background in show business and good connections with managers and agents (rather than the celebrities themselves) and these are the people who will contact you. The famous only appear on chat shows because they have something to promote – their latest movie, record, book or business venture. If they have recently been the subject of scandalous revelations, they may want to put their side of the story, which is effectively promoting their image.

There needs to be a good mix of people on programmes in order to maximize the audience. If you have three sportsmen, movie-goers will not tune in. If you have three actors, sports fans will stay away. There will also be problems with promotion, because all three will want top billing.

It is usual to meet the celebrity before the recording/transmission. Of course, the researcher must find out as much background information as possible before the meeting. The best source is newspaper cuttings. Use what the agent supplies to supplement your reading and, if it is a book that is being promoted, read as much of it as you can. Be aware, however, that not only do many celebrities not write the books that bear their name, they may not even have read them.

If you are dealing with someone who has recently become famous and is not accustomed to the media, you must assess how well they will come across. On radio, this is less important because interviews can easily be edited, but for television, you need to get some idea, perhaps from a local radio appearance.

Information about structuring and carrying out a research interview is given on pp. 62–65. As well as discussing what can be asked on the show, it is essential to discover what the celebrity will not talk about. Chat shows are not in the business of conducting trials. Managers and agents, however, may want to vet the questions to be asked and may even want to know the precise wording. Here you run into problems of editorial control, so you need to know your company's policy on this and be prepared to negotiate with the person's representative.

Contestant research

This is another specialist area. Some companies making quiz and game shows have a standard form for potential contestants, others have a telephone line. You will also get a good response from social clubs and the regional offices of large companies. If you are working on a quiz show that requires specialist rather than general knowledge, you can also advertise in the kind of publication potential contestants are likely to read. You will probably get more applicants than you can interview.

In radio, assessing the potential contestant's level of knowledge is usually carried out on the telephone, but for television researchers usually arrange a series of regional interviews of those whose application forms and photographs suggest these are the kind of people the show needs. This is cheaper than paying their fares to come to your city. Choose a hotel in a place where there are good transport facilities so that people in small villages can travel easily. As well as your own accommodation, you will need another room in which to carry out the interviews.

People should be interviewed in groups so you can see how outgoing they are. Then a round of questions where they compete to answer will gauge their level of knowledge, speed of reaction and help weed out those who behave inappropriately if they lose or win. Note this information on their application forms – this helps to cut down on the amount of paperwork.

At the end of your interviews, you will have a file of suitable contestants. Now you can sort them into individual programmes to get a good mix of sex, age, social background and region. Putting older people with those who are much younger is a mistake because their reaction times tend to be slower and, however good their knowledge, they will be beaten to the buzzer. The aim is not to find the winner of the programme, but to make sure that all contestants have an equal chance to maintain audience interest.

Most shows are recorded in blocks. Arranging transport and accommodation for them is usually the researcher's job. As well as those booked to appear, there must be a few on standby in case of emergencies or illness. It is also worth having a reserve list of people living near where the recording takes place in case of transport or weather problems.

In television, plain black, white, red and cream clothes and those with small stripes and checks cause visual problems so contestants need to be warned not to wear them. If the winner goes on to the next round, they will also need a change of clothes. A few outfits from the Costume Department need to be available just in case.

Specialist contributor research

Recording interviews

A research interview is conducted to check the contributors' suitability and to assess the kind of contribution they can make to the programme. In television it is usual to meet contributors before they are recorded, except if they are already experienced in appearing on screen or for current affairs programmes which have a very short timescale. In these situations, there may only be a telephone call to decide how well the contributor will come across either in a recording or a studio appearance.

With inexperienced interviewees, the aim of the research interview is partly to find out what kind of contribution they can make and partly to see them. In an ideal world, it would not matter what people look like, but viewers will be distracted from what is being said if the interviewee has an unusual appearance or some physical mannerism, such as a facial tic.

It is also an opportunity to gauge how the interviewee is likely to react to being recorded. However, there is no foolproof method of knowing who will be intimidated by recording and who will sail through it, no matter how confident they appear when you talk to them.

The method of recording the interview must be decided. See the chart opposite for the methods and their pros and cons.

Methods of recording

METHOD	ADVANTAGES	DISADVANTAGES
Writing notes	Good for the occasional fact especially over the phone	Breaks personal contact with interviewee
	Non-mechanical, so not offputting	Connotations of 'Anything you say may be taken down and used in evidence ...'
Tape recording	Accurate record of what was said	Interviewee may be self-conscious May take a long time to find what you need when listening back
Video camera	Accurate record of how the interviewee will come across on screen	Breaks personal contact with interviewees
		Interviewees may feel they have done the interview, so when you return with a full crew, you get a dull response
	Good for locations to see what the camera will see	
Still camera/ Polaroid	Good for locations and objects	Possible lack of picture quality
Memory	Maintains personal contact with interviewee	Inaccuracy
	Saves time because you do not have to listen back to the recording and what you find interesting, the audience	No proof of what was said

Preparing to interview

The research meeting has two purposes – the first is effectively to audition potential contributors for a television programme or video production; but the second is to gain their confidence.

Dress, posture and manner will all contribute to the impression you and the production are creating.

Decide what to wear. You need to look professional, but not intimidating. The idea should be to show interviewees that you have considered who they are and for some people casual clothes will be appropriate. Dress should not be too casual and never wear anything that is less than spotlessly clean. When in doubt, dress up slightly to show an effort has been made. Where is the meeting to be? Is your footwear suitable if you are going to be outside, for example on a building site or in a garden?

Your manner must also be appropriate. You will already have gained some impression about the interviewee from telephone conversations. If you are meeting a busy tycoon, brisk professionalism should be the keynote to show that you recognize time is valuable. A gentler, less dynamic approach is needed to talk to someone unused to interviews or on a sensitive subject.

Find out how to get there and how long the journey is likely to take. Turning up late is one of the worst things you can do. It looks unprofessional, may inconvenience the interviewees and suggests that you do not consider their needs to be important.

If you are travelling a long distance, there is a lot to be said for using public transport. You can use time spent on trains (both outward and return) to work. Local taxi drivers will know the area so you will not arrive in a flustered state if you have had trouble finding the place.

Although you will already have done some research into the subject, you may need to do more and consider carefully what you want from the meeting and structure it. Think of an interview as a conversation, but a conversation with a point. In social situations, you might find yourself meeting someone about whom you have already heard a great deal. In general, you do not plunge into the most interesting and scandalous aspect immediately. It is the same for research interviews. Lead up to the important questions gradually.

Structuring the interview

Conversations, job interviews, research interviews for television – even some police interviews of suspects – all follow a similar structure. There is usually a little of what in linguistics is called 'phatic communion', such as 'Hello', 'Nice weather' and 'Did you have a good journey?' These do not convey information, but are designed to signal good will and to gain the trust of the person. Obviously, you do not have to script these in advance, but you do need to think about the kind of questions you will ask in the main part of the interview and the order in which you will ask them.

Factual answers are easy for the interviewee to answer, so the interview proper starts off with them. This is not a waste of time, as it will help to confirm, refute or add to research already done. When the interviewee has gained confidence and trust, you can go on to areas that are more speculative or which involve beliefs, emotions and opinions. You may also need to prepare in advance the exact phrasing of particular questions, especially those which are on sensitive matters.

Closed/open questions

Closed questions are those that lead to a one-word answer. They are more useful to clarify something or at the recording stage (see p. 118) when you know what you want the interviewee to talk about. If you use them too much in a research interview, you may miss something that is important to the story. Asking 'Has any research been done on this?' might elicit the answer 'No' If, however, you ask, 'What kind of research has been done on this?', the interviewee may say that nothing on this particular area has been done but quite a lot on a related subject. This opens up two further avenues to explore: why has nothing been done and what are the implications of the work on the related area.

Open questions invite the interviewee to give a fuller answer. They start with what journalists call the 6 Ws: Who ... , What ... , Why ... , When ... , How ... , Where ... ? To this list, you can add Tell me about ... . All such questions allow the interviewee to select what he or she wants to tell you. If you get the impression there is more, you can encourage interviewees to go on by repeating their last few words as a question, e.g.

INTERVIEWEE: '...and the traders just got it wrong.' (PAUSES)
INTERVIEWER: 'They got it wrong?'
INTERVIEWEE: 'Yes, they thought it meant prices would go up.'
INTERVIEWER: 'Why was that?'

Consider how different phrasing will affect the answer:

- 'What do you think will happen . . .?'
- 'What do you feel will happen . . .?'
- 'How do you see the situation developing . . .?'

The reply to each of these will have subtle differences. The first question invites a reasoned analysis, the second a gut reaction and the third a speculative forecast. Once you have started each area of interest with an open question, you can then follow up by asking questions requiring a more precise answer, perhaps by offering alternatives such as 'Does this mean . . .?' or something that does require a simple 'Yes' or 'No'. However, these should not be prepared in advance. When the interview takes place, you should be listening and thinking about the implications.

Practical considerations

If you are using a tape recorder, check that it works. You should know how to operate such equipment. If you are worried about the tape recorder, you will not concentrate on the interview and you will create the wrong impression. If you are making written notes, does your pen work or have you got enough pencils? Will you need to take any other equipment, for example a camera for location shots?

As well as the recording equipment you will be using, you need to consider what else might be useful, depending on the kind of person you are meeting and the purpose of the interview. You might want to take photographs with you if you are asking people about the past, in order to trigger their memories. When you are conducting a potentially contentious interview, it is a good idea to take press cuttings or other sources of information which might be needed to prove where you got your information.

Sometimes it is necessary to set up interviews a week or so in advance. Things can change in that time, so call the day before to check that the interviewee is still available, especially if you are travelling a long distance.

Before you set off, check that you have got:

- the recording equipment
- spare cassettes and batteries or pens/pencils
- details of how to get there
- contact telephone numbers
- change or a telephone card in case you lose your mobile or it does not work and, if you are driving, for parking meters
- if appropriate (for women) a spare pair of tights.

Planning an interview checklist

Decide:

- what you need to know
- what kind of questions to ask at each stage of the interview
- the best way of recording the interview
- what to wear
- how to get there.

Interview stages

1 Phatic communion (to establish a rapport and put them at their ease).
2 Factual information (to give them confidence and for you to check your facts).
3 Key questions (the main purpose of the interview).
4 Factual information, such as availability and expenses. (This allows them to return to normal and feel good about the experience.)

Conducting a research interview

Follow the structure you have already prepared, but do not work rigidly down your list of questions or areas for discussion. Pursue interesting sidelines without losing sight of all the points to be covered. However, try not to make it too obvious that there is a list. Remember that this is a conversation and the relationship you should be building up with the interviewee will be jeopardized if you keep consulting a piece of paper. If a tape recorder is being used, put it to one side, not between you and the interviewee and then, as far as possible, forget about it.

Although the aim is to hold a conversation, the interviewee is the most important factor. Your views and experiences are, generally, not of interest and you may alienate or irritate the person you are talking to if you express them. There are exceptions to this. If you are working on a sensitive subject, interviewees may be more forthcoming if they know you share or can understand their experiences.

Do not argue with interviewees, however misguided, repulsive or just plain wrong what they say is. You might need to suggest that there are opposing views to elicit responses, but this must be phrased neutrally. Consider carefully which sources of information or views you choose to quote. On the other hand, be careful about expressing agreement. If both sides of an argument are to be included in the final programme, contributors may feel betrayed if they were led to believe only their views would be represented.

Body language
Body language and posture are important when you meet the interviewee. Hunching yourself defensively with crossed arms does not promote an atmosphere of trust. Sprawling backwards with your arms and legs spread out does not, however, suggest ease but superiority. Be careful that you do not betray boredom or impatience by looking round the room, trying to glance covertly at your watch (it never works, people always know) or shuffling your feet.

If you are carrying a bulging briefcase or a lot of paraphernalia, try to leave it outside the room where you are doing the interview, along with your overcoat, scarf, hat or other extraneous clothing. These might suggest that you are too rushed to give the interviewee your full attention and they will make you look like a stranger.

You can pick up a lot of clues about how the interviewee is feeling through their body language. As well as the actions mentioned earlier, feeling under pressure can be suspected if they are shifting around in their seats. Touching their noses or putting their hands in front of their mouths suggests they might be lying. However, care needs to be taken when drawing conclusions from body language. It may simply be that the seat is uncomfortable; that the person has an itchy nose or is self-conscious about ugly teeth. Do not focus on one event, but look at behaviour as a whole.

Body language

Sitting hunched up, with arms crossed defensively, does not create an atmosphere of trust.

Sprawling backwards suggests superiority, not relaxation.

Getting a good story

Much of the time you will be talking to ordinary people about their experiences. If you are making a recording for a radio programme, you need to get the interviewee to tell you exactly what you want for the final programme. However, if you are conducting a preliminary research interview and you will be coming back later with a full crew to record the final contribution, you do not actually want the interviewee to tell you everything now. You have to leave something in reserve for the final recording.

Only professional actors can repeat a performance – ordinary people do not say exactly the same thing each time they tell a story. If you get all the details of something that happened to them at the research interview stage, when you come to the final recording you will find the person has nothing in reserve. This means that you need to be very careful when doing the research interview not to let the person tell the whole story so it needs a great deal of care and experience to avoid appearing callous or dismissive of what is important to them.

Active listening

Whatever the purpose of the interview, there is a technique known as 'active listening' which helps to both establish a good relationship with the interviewees and to ensure that you are getting what they say right. Feed back to the interviewees a summary of what you understand them to have said using slightly different words.

This needs care to avoid putting words in their mouth or directing the interview in a way that might not be a fair representation of the interviewee's position, especially in controversial or sensitive areas. Someone who feels they have been badly treated can be further inflamed if you say, for example, 'You must have been really angry . . . how awful' and then 'I suppose, you felt really betrayed . . .'. This is unethical.

Winding up

The interview will probably come to a natural conclusion. It is not a good idea to leap up, switch off the tape recorder and depart immediately you have got a good, emotional story or a controversial opinion. You do not want to leave potential contributors in a highly wrought state, wondering if they have said too much or the wrong thing to someone who is, after all, a stranger from the media. They must feel secure and, of course, trust you. So go back to factual matters.

Check you can come back if you need any further information and on availability for the final recording, without committing yourself to a definite agreement that the interviewee will appear. This might be the right time to ask people to reconsider any requests made for anonymity or for certain things to be off-the-record. You will have gained an impression about how best to phrase this kind of request and they, in turn, should have made up their minds about your trustworthiness.

Conducting an interview checklist

Do:

- wear suitable clothes and footwear
- turn up on time
- turn off your mobile phone
- keep your body language relaxed and be aware of theirs
- keep control of the interview
- maintain eye contact, unless the person is from a culture in which this is impolite
- listen
- ask open questions
- ask clear, simple questions
- thank them for their time and write a thank you note afterwards
- play devil's advocate to get an impassioned response, but be polite.

Do not:

- ask clever questions
- ask closed questions
- ask double questions
- ask them so much detail that by the time the recording happens they have given their performance
- argue on a personal basis
- lose your temper
- interrupt
- give your own opinions.

Conducting an interview for radio

Almost all the points about conducting a research interview (see pp. 58–61) apply here, but there are one or two differences because what you are producing is the final recording, rather than a preliminary meeting.

Although those working on audio-visual productions almost always need to meet interviewees, this is not necessary with radio. Thus, you might find it more convenient to record a telephone interview (this is more common with news programmes) or to make what is called a 'down the line' recording from another radio studio, which means booking lines in advance. If you decide to record a telephone interview because, perhaps, you only need a short piece, make sure the interviewee knows it is being recorded (this is a regulation).

You need to plan your questions and structure the interview very carefully. If the interviewee gives an interesting answer, but takes 5 minutes to do it and you only want 2, try asking them to say it again. Alternatively, you can suggest the need for concision by your questions, for example 'In a few words, why . . .?' and 'Can you sum that up?'

Body language

The main difference is what you say must not overlap with what the interviewee is saying. Therefore, you cannot encourage the interviewee by saying 'Yes, I see' or something similar while they are speaking. Nor can you murmur 'Mmm' encouragingly. You have only your facial expression and body language to show that you comprehend and are interested.

An increasing number of people in official positions are going on media training courses that teach them to have their say, regardless of all the hints the interviewer is dropping. If you do not want to interrupt, you can speed them up by your body language, breaking eye contact, opening your mouth as if you are about to speak (but not actually saying anything which would cause editing problems), shifting in your chair and so on. In extreme cases, you can try peering at the tape recorder with a worried expression to suggest that their words are not being recorded for posterity.

Conducting radio interviews checklist

Will you record:

- face to face
- over the telephone
- down the line from another studio?

Will your questions be included in the final programme?

Is there background sound that might irritate or puzzle the listener, for example:

- air conditioning (ask for it to be turned off)
- ticking/chiming clocks (put them in another room or, if this is not possible, record elsewhere)
- anything the interviewee is wearing that makes a noise when they move (e.g. jewellery or leather clothes)
- plastic or leather chairs which squeak when you or the interviewee moves?
- background music which will cause editing problems (ask for it to be turned off, if possible, or record elsewhere).

Listen to what the interviewee is saying and:

- follow up interesting leads by asking supplementary questions
- ask for jargon or technical terms to be explained
- make sure that what they are saying does not contravene the law, for example by expressing a defamatory opinion
- make sure that what they are saying is factually accurate.

Tips

- Check that the interview has recorded before leaving.
- Never say, 'Finally . . .'. You may want to use a different final question when you come to edit and it will waste time to re-record your question.

After the interview

However you have chosen to record the interview – on tape, by making notes or just relying on your memory – you will need to add to this as soon as possible after the interview has finished. How does the person come across, were there any points at which body language told you something the words did not? If you are interviewing several people in a day, make notes on each instantly – you may think that you will remember, but immediate impressions can be blurred by subsequent conversations.

Next day, or as soon as possible, write to the interviewee. Depending on the situation and the person, you should write either a letter, perhaps confirming any arrangements you might have made (but see next page), or a brief note thanking them for their time. You will know best whether it is more appropriate to send a typed communication or a few words handwritten on a card or post-card. The latter is quicker to do. If you keep a stack of postcards in your desk drawer, it takes very little time to scribble a brief thank-you and put it in an envelope. The people you deal with are usually surprised and delighted to have such a personal acknowledgement and it helps to build up the relationship you are creating between contributor and production.

Writing up a research interview
If you have done a research interview which will later be recorded by a full crew, the whole interview or part of it may need to be transcribed. Alternatively, a summary of what was said, noting any particular points of interest, may be enough. Add your impressions of the person and suggestions about how the interviewee could be used which you can discuss later with the rest of the team. Highlight any good anecdotes or opinions that can be elicited at the recording.

Issuing contracts to contributors
When it has been decided which contributors are to be used in the programme, the circumstances associated with their appearance will have to be agreed. Sometimes this is just done on the telephone or by a simple, standard form, letter or fax. Alternatively, a special contract may need to be drawn up, especially if an actor or a musician to whom union rates may apply is being used. If there are special arrangements to be made, it is best to put them in writing.

Before transmission
You need to let contributors know when the programme they are involved in is going out. This is partly a matter of good manners and partly a way of maximizing the audience (they will tell many other people). It can be done either by passing names and addresses to the person on the team who is dealing with the task or, if this person is you, keeping a separate list. When potential contributors are recorded but do not appear in the final production, it is still important to let them know. They have almost certainly put themselves to some trouble to help you and you may need their help again in future. Phrase such letters carefully – don't send a bland, standard formula of the 'regrettably, there was not enough time to include your contribution' kind. Also, if you can, sign it personally, rather than have it signed on your behalf by an assistant or secretary.

Matters for consideration and confirmation, either verbally or in writing, are:

- fee (if any) and expenses
- dates and details of the appearance or recording, the time and place
- whether transport will be provided or whether the interviewees must make their own arrangements (you may need to organize parking spaces, if they are coming in their own cars)
- if the interviewee needs to stay overnight, you may have to organize accommodation
- consent – your contributor may need permission to appear (special arrangements apply to children, especially if they are to give a performance)
- health and safety, including any special facilities that have to be organized (e.g. wheelchair access and protective clothing).

Vox pops

Vox pops comes from the Latin *vox populi*, which means 'the voice of the people'. It is the term used for the process of going out into the street and asking passers-by for quick comments on a current issue, to test a product or make a brief contribution to the programme in some way.

As it is not a full interview, no telephone calls need to be made nor full-scale research interviews done in advance, but you do need to put some careful thought into what you are going to do, especially if you are asking a question which must be simple to prevent incomprehension or misunderstanding.

You also need to choose your location carefully. Where are you most likely to find the type of contribution you need – a shopping centre or market, city street or wine bar, outside the local school gates or a college? What is the best time to go to find the people you need? You will probably have to get permission to film there as well (see pp. 92–95).

Vox pops are never done singly. You need a number of them that are cut together in a sequence. This is a situation where you really must ensure a variety of people. The team and crew turn up in a likely location to pick individuals to contribute. The researcher approaches the person, says what is required and asks if she or he would like to contribute. If you are asking a question, do not put it to the interviewees at this stage because they will have lost all spontaneity when it comes to do the actual recording and the result will be tired and flat. Instead, tell them the subject of the interview and, if you will be asking that kind of question, find out if they are for or against. This is partly so you get a representative selection of pros and cons and partly so the director knows how to shoot them. The convention is to have people of different opinions facing different ways.

Stereotypes are useful here – if people say what you would expect them to from their appearance, the audience will think smugly 'I knew they would say that.' If their views do not match what the audience expects, their reaction will be one of surprise. Either way, you cannot lose.

You should also make sure that you get all the interviewees to sign a basic contract giving your programme the rights to the interview. This prevents problems later if they have second thoughts about their contribution. In addition, should the company want to sell the programme or part of it on, it will have to prove that it has cleared all the rights in the content, which includes even contributions that last a few seconds.

Vox pops checklist

- Make the question simple.
- Ask people the same question so it will edit together well.
- If you are asking people to agree/disagree with your question, shoot them from different sides – those who agree facing one way, those who disagree the other. Even if you do not want opinions, make sure they are not all facing the same way.
- Too many is boring; too few may mean you do not make your point.

Tips

- Choose a wide variety of people of different sexes, ages, ethnic origins, etc.
- Choose a location suitable for the question, but remember that people in a hurry (e.g. running for a train) will not be co-operative or eloquent.
- Pick a good reply for the end – a short, amusing, snappy answer.
- Rephrase the question if you are not getting a good response.

Vox pops

Using archive material

Although information and people remain the bedrock of all news and documentary programmes, there is a limit to the number of talking heads the viewer or listener will endure. Television requires a variety of visual elements to sustain interest. The maxim here is show rather than tell, so as well as archive footage, think about graphics and objects. Radio has to rely on audio material to achieve its effects. Although sound is often low on the list of considerations in television, it can enhance a production considerably.

The audience may need to see, or hear, an event or situation rather than have it described to them. Archive footage of, for example, an event in the past will add to understanding of the event – remember the journalists' dictum 'Every picture is worth a thousand words.' The sound of an air-raid siren recaptures the atmosphere of wartime for older people. The way people talk has changed considerably within the last 30 years – footage of people speaking, either on film or sound alone, is a reminder of what people thought and how they expressed those thoughts in the past.

Even on a documentary programme, a voice-over either by a narrator or by the subject of the programme recorded on wild-track containing factual information will be better than just a talking head. So, rather than seeing an elderly woman say she was born in Leeds in the 1930s, the eldest of six children, you should consider getting archive film of Leeds at that time, perhaps with children playing in the street, and lay her voice giving these factual details over it. Alternatively, there might be a still photograph of her family you could use.

Some programmes use footage from television companies around the world, not only to report current events but to demonstrate how funny foreign footage can be. Others use amateur recordings of domestic disasters. Again, the original must be obtained – simply describing what happened or re-enacting it in the studio would not produce the same effect of authenticity.

There may not be the time to film events or a place may currently be inaccessible for political reasons. This applies in particular to news, which uses a great deal of archive footage called up from a library. Distance may also be a consideration and sometimes this is a matter of convenience, sometimes it is a question of expense.

It may be too expensive to send a film crew or a photographer to a place, but library footage or stills of, for example, South America will show everything from Aztec temples to current living conditions there.

Acquiring material

The next decision to be made is whether to buy, license or commission. This is all to do with rights rather than the material itself.

- **Buying material** Buying the right to use something is the most straightforward way of acquisition, but is not always possible. Libraries make their living from licensing material – they are not going to give lightly up a potential source of income. If, however, you are getting something from a private source, try to buy the right for its use outright. It will make repeats and sales elsewhere much easier.
- **Licensing material** Licensing is, in effect, hiring the material for a specific purpose. The production signs a contract with the organization or person owning the material to use it under certain conditions, which usually include the number of times it may be shown, in which parts of the world or territories it may be shown and what fee will be payable. This will depend on the type of production and size of the potential audience. Something to be broadcast on one of the mass media channels will attract a higher cost than a video intended for training purposes within a few companies. In general, costs for educational programmes are lower. This is a complex area. If only short inserts presenting few problems are required, however, this will fall within the remit of general programme research. If the film research required is extensive or might present problems, a specialist should be used.
- **Commissioning material** This method is especially useful for still photographs and music. For reasons explained on pp. 122–129, it may be impossible or too expensive to get the rights to the material you want. If you hire a photographer to take still photographs or musicians to compose and/or record the music you need, then your production will own the rights so there are no difficulties about using them. Ensure that the contract notes that the production retains the copyright on the work produced. In some situations, it might be preferable, or even necessary, to hire an artist to draw a picture. This is most common when reporting court cases in countries where cameras of any kind are not allowed at trials.

Film and videotape libraries

Film has been around since 1895 and, in the more than 100 years since its invention, literally millions of feet of film have been recorded and stored in a variety of places.

There are large, general archives – both national and regional – as well as commercial libraries. Some specialize in what is called stock footage, that is, clips of generic subjects such as aeroplanes, animals or countries. These are useful when specially shot footage is either too expensive or too inconvenient to obtain. There are also the archives of newsreel companies which used to produce the short packages that formed a standard part of cinema programmes until the 1970s. Before the advent of television, the cinema was where people went to see the news both in the UK and abroad. Specialist archives collect footage on a particular subject, such as transport.

Other archives may be contained within a larger institution, such as a museum, which will also hold still photographs and objects. Commercial companies such as chain stores and trade unions may have their own archives. Local history libraries often have films made by local amateurs and there are also individual collectors and amateur film-makers.

Most of the libraries have rate cards, which give details of the costs involved in using their material. Time spent browsing through them and other information about film and videotape archives as well as getting to know the staff is not wasted. The more knowledge a researcher holds in his or her head, the less time will be wasted looking for it in printed sources, or making a series of fruitless telephone calls, often against the clock.

Dealing with overseas archives brings additional complications, not just because the records will be in another language, but also because working hours may be different. Time zones and British Summer Time also need to be taken into account. For example, the United States is between 5 and 11 hours behind Britain. If you want something from Australia (which is between 7 and 11 hours ahead), you may have to call in your own time.

It is also worth remembering that US libraries usually charge more than their counterparts, so always see if the clip you want has been recorded by a cheaper country.

A chart should be prepared to keep track of the material being used. As a minimum, it should include the date of the footage, the duration of clip, the content in the form of a shot list, the source, the copyright owner, the format, details of transfer (including the spool number), cost and miscellaneous information, such as restrictions on use.

Damaged film can be repaired and scratches removed digitally, but the process can be long and therefore expensive. For short clips, the time and money involved may not be worth the effort, but it is worth considering if the flawed piece you have plays an important part in the programme. Find out how much it will cost and check if the budget will allow the work to be done.

Specific footage

Where you go to get your archive footage depends on whether you need a specific event or just a general illustration of what is being said. If you must have a specific event, you should start with the newsreel libraries or television companies' archives. Although most now have computerized indices to their collections, you may need to find at least an approximate date. Perhaps you are working on a programme about a man who later became famous and who was once recorded for a vox pop about tattoos. It is unlikely that his name was noted at the time. Even something as vague as 'It was the year Argentina won the World Cup' will give you a starting point. Newspaper indices would be useful here if no-one in the office is a football fan.

It is worth thinking about overseas sources as well – something that might not have been important enough for your own country to send a film crew may have been of greater importance there and so would have been filmed.

Wallpaper

News bulletins on television may need general rather than specific footage. This is known as wallpaper – moving pictures over which the news item is read. It is not quite a question of 'never mind the quality, measure the length', but often it is a matter of getting whatever is already available in the company's library or can be quickly obtained featuring the subject of the news item. Stock footage of aeroplanes taking off, traffic jams, etc. is also useful here.

Still picture libraries

Picture libraries hold colour and black and white photographs, either prints or negatives from which a print will have to be made and paid for, whether it is included or not in the final production. Many also have transparencies. Check which is the most suitable format to obtain, depending on the way the picture is to be used.

If only part of the picture is to be featured or a move across it in a simple way is needed, this can be done on location or in the studio with a cameraman/woman at the same time as the rest of the recording. When something more complicated, such as changing the colour or co-ordinating camera movements with music, is needed, specialist rostrum camera facilities will have to be booked and the pictures taken there. In news programmes and for doing some graphics sequences a slide scanner may be used. This is a fixed electronic camera which projects, as the name implies, transparencies.

Check how the pictures will be used and where in the production they will be included. Newspaper photographs are intended to add information to the printed text or even sum up the whole story. News programmes in particular may need something less dramatic, just a head-and-shoulders, studio portrait of a person as a visual reminder of who is being mentioned. A detailed photograph would distract viewers from what is being said. Alternatively, an informal picture may be needed to illustrate something in the script. The sentence 'He and his second wife met at a party given by Scott and Zelda Fitzgerald in Paris' would need to show the couple at a party, ideally with one or both of the Fitzgeralds. In an ideal world, of course, moving pictures would be best for this situation.

It is always better to go along to a library if at all possible. However well the context is explained to the librarian or researcher there, she or he will not have the detailed knowledge of where and how a still is going to be included. Libraries have different ways of working – some allow people to take a selection of pictures away with them, others require prints (which will have to be paid for) to be made from negatives.

Keeping track of pictures, especially if your production is using a large number, is essential. A chart must be prepared, listing the picture, the source, the date it was taken, the copyright owner (who may not be the library, so check this), the fee, where and how the picture is to be used, the spool number of any tape on which it is recorded and other miscellaneous information, such as restrictions on use. These are the minimum requirements for the list, although the actual content and layout will vary to include precisely the knowledge you and the production need. Cardboard-backed envelopes to keep prints undamaged are essential. Restoring damaged pictures can easily be done by computer.

Using archive material checklist

- Why is archive material needed? Is it for authenticity, convenience or expense?
- What kind of material is needed? Is it moving pictures, still pictures or sound?
- is it a specific event or wallpaper?
- How is the material to be acquired? Is it through buying or licensing?
- If buying or licensing are too expensive, how much will it cost to commission?

Checking names

If you have a still (or footage) taken from a library of someone with a very common name, check that she or he does not share that name with another person in public life both when ordering the material and when it is delivered. Ensure that the script distinguishes between them, if necessary. You also need to check the spelling. For example, there is an actor Anthony Hopkins and a composer Antony Hopkins.

Still picture libraries

Film formats

When obtaining film or videotape footage, always ask in which formats the library holds the material. There may be a choice, so you can obtain a copy that can be incorporated into your production with a minimum of complicated or expensive transfer time. It should be established early on which facilities will have to be specially booked and how much they will cost.

The main film formats a non-specialist researcher is likely to encounter are 35 mm, 16 mm, Super 16 and Super 8. Earlier, there were a variety of formats (see opposite), but most of the experimentation was used for feature films. Copies for cinemas or amateur film societies, which had very basic equipment, may also have been made.

Film can come with the sound on a separate magnetic track (sep-mag) or with the sound on a strip running alongside the pictures (com-opt). The former is easier to use if it needs to be heavily edited or a new commentary is going to be put on something which already contains music or sound effects. Ask if there is a separate music and effects (M&E) track. If the sound has been mixed down to leave only one track with words, music and effects all together (as it is in com-opt prints), it is virtually impossible to isolate the different elements and delete one of them. However, for a short, simple clip, com-opt film is better.

Before 1951, professional 35 mm film was recorded on nitrate stock, which is highly flammable and special arrangements have to be made for its transfer. After that date, safety stock was used by professionals. It had been used for amateur footage (16 mm or 8 mm) from the beginning, but its tendency to warp made it unsuitable for professional use. Most commercial libraries have now transferred their nitrate stock footage to less flammable material, but you may still find some, either in libraries or in private hands, and you should be aware of its problems.

Film formats

DATE	SIZE	NOTES
1895	51 mm	Widescreen format.
1898+	17.5 mm	
1900	75 mm	Lumiere
1904		*Sprockets began to be punched by manufacturer, rather than the customer*
1909	35 mm	Edison format adopted as standard
1912	28 mm	Reduced from 35 mm
1914	70 mm	Panoramica, later reduced to horizontal 35 mm
1923	9.5 mm	
1923	16 mm	
1927	35 mm	Cinamascope, used anamorphic lens requiring special projection and transfer facilities
1927	35 mm	Polyvision, 2 × 35 mm frames projected simultaneously
1932	8 mm	Amateur format
1937		*Television began in Britain. It could use film shot with a conventional camera, passed immediately through the developing process, then scanned and transmitted in under a minute. Few recordings of early, live transmissions survive.*
1951	35 mm	Safety stock for professional use introduced and universally adopted almost immediately
	Super 8	Mainly an amateur format
1958		*Telerecording, a method of recording the output of an electronic studio on to film, introduced. Some programmes survive only in this form.*
1960	3 mm	USAF, used in space
1968		*Colour television began*
1990	Super 16	Uses 40% more image area than standard 16 mm

Note: In the early days, there were experiments with a number of different sizes, which continued even after the Edison format had been adopted as standard.

Videotape formats

Early videotape imitated film in that it came on an open reel. When transferring these, extra time must be allowed to set them up. Videotape now comes on cassette in a number of formats both for professional and domestic use. Companies tend to acquire equipment that is state-of-the-art when the time comes to refit their studios or edit suites, but they do not necessarily change everything when a new system comes along. The chart opposite shows the date when the more common formats first became available. However, remember that some organizations may still be using a format invented 15 years or more ago.

In addition to those shown, there were many others which appeared briefly or were confined to one particular market. In the early 1970s there were three 1" helical scan formats produced by competing manufacturers (Shabaden, Sony and Phillips), which were used mainly for closed-circuit television in educational establishments. So if you are working on a programme about someone who was a teacher and might have been recorded, bear this in mind.

There is a further sub-division, namely whether it is analogue or digital. Reproduction of the former deteriorates with each generation of copies made. The latter does not degrade because is it based on numbers, which remain the same for each generation, rather than copying a signal. This may be an important consideration if extensive editing on linear equipment is required.

Technical information with the videotape should say whether there are separate tracks for commentary and music and effects (M&E).

All these problems – both for film and video – mean anyone doing research must ask which format the original material is on and then either know or find out the facilities that are needed to transfer it.

YEAR	FORMAT	SIGNAL	ON	SIZE	NOTES
1956	2"	Analogue	Open reel	2"	Also known as Quad; cannot be viewed while spooling backwards and forwards
1969	U-matic hi-band	Analogue	Cassette	¾"	Used for Electronic News Gathering (ENG)
1969	U-matic lo-band	Analogue	Cassette	¾"	Used for off-line editing
1969	U-matic hi-band SP	Analogue	Cassette	¾"	
1971	1" B format	Analogue	Open reel	1"	
1972	1" C format	Analogue	Open reel	1"	
1976	VHS	Analogue	Cassette	½"	Domestic format
1985	Betacam	Analogue	Cassette	½"	Used for Portable Single Camera (PSC) recording on location
1987	D1	Digital	Cassette	¾"	
1988	D2	Digital	Cassette	¾"	
1988	S-VHS	Analogue	Cassette	½"	Domestic format
1989	Hi-8	Analogue	Cassette	½"	Domestic format
1989	Betacam SP	Analogue	Cassette	½"	
1990	D3	Digital	Cassette	½"	
1992	DCT	Digital	Cassette	¾"	Mainly used for post-production
1992	DCT	Digital	Open reel	1"	
1993	D5	Digital	Cassette	½"	
1994	Digital Betacam	Digital	Cassette	½"	
1996	DVC	Digital	Cassette	½"	
1996	DVC Pro	Digital	Cassette	¼"	
1996	Mini-DVC	Digital	Cassette	¼"	
1996	Digital S	Digital	Cassette	½"	
1996	Sony DV	Digital	Cassette	¼"	
1997	Betacam SX	Digital	Cassette	¼"	

Note: HDCAM (Sony), HDD5 and DVCPRO-HD (Panasonic) have been developed as high resolution television broadcast formats, which are usually referred to as high definition television (HDTV).

Videotape formats

Television standards and aspect ratios

Television standards

If material from overseas is being used, the different television standards used in other parts of the world must be taken into account. Currently there are three. They have different line standards, which is also a consideration when using old videotape. Early material comes mostly from transfers to film and is of poor quality, but some videotape with better picture quality survives. It was also black and white.

NAME OF SYSTEM	MAJOR USERS	NO. OF FRAMES PER SECOND	NO. OF LINES
Phase Alternating Line (PAL)	Great Britain, most of Europe, Australia, New Zealand, China, India, Anglophone Africa	25	625
National Televison Systems Committee (NTSC)	United States, Canada, Japan, Anglophone Caribbean	24	525
Sequence Couleur à Memoire (Secam V)	France, Francophone Africa, Francophone Caribbean	25	625

Note: There are developments of these standards, such as PAL M (used in Brazil and Laos), PAL N (in Argentina), Secam H (used in Greece, Mongolia and Eastern Europe). Some countries use two, for example China uses PAL and NTSC.

Aspect ratios

The aspect ratio between the width and height of a screen is different in the cinema from that used in television. The original cinema ratio was 4:3 and analogue television adopted this. Later the cinema developed and used widescreen and Cinemascope ratios. When showing some feature films on television, a black band appears at the top and bottom of the screen. This is called 'letterboxing'. This can be corrected on transfer but there is some loss of the picture. In digital broadcasting the aspect ratio is 16:9 so using clips from early television programmes or feature films also presents problems. The choice is to stretch pictures, which leads to distortion, or to have blank strips around the sides.

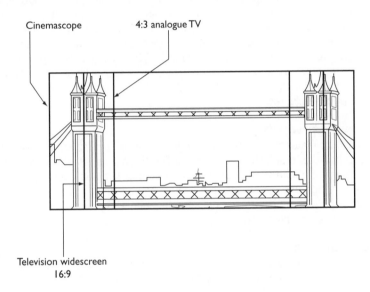

Cinemascope   4:3 analogue TV

Television widescreen
16:9

Sound

There are three kinds of recorded sound:

- music
- spoken word
- sound effects.

Music

The problems here are not so much technical as financial and are largely to do with copyright. Although it can be expensive, this is an area where commissioning a composer and a group of musicians to achieve what you want is worth considering. National archives, such as the British Library National Sound Archive, may not only collect pre-recorded music, but also have a programme of actively recording musical performances. This includes the spoken word (e.g. poetry readings and theatrical plays) and particular kinds of sound (e.g. wildlife). However, they may not hold the rights to performances, which will still have to be cleared.

The spoken word

In addition to material available from sound archives, a number of local history projects have an oral history group recording the memories of people in their area. However, these are usually on domestic quality audio cassettes so may not be of a high enough standard to use for broadcasting. In such a case, the project organizers may be able to put you in touch with people from the project whom you can re-interview.

Sound effects

These are readily available on records and CDs. They are copyrighted but, like mood music, present relatively few clearance problems. If the effect you want is unusual or highly specialized, commissioning should also be considered. The authentic sound of something may not be very impressive and may have to be recreated by the most unlikely means. Footsteps may need to be dubbed on to your production because the sync sound did not produce the desired effect. Getting a commercial recording to match exactly is unlikely. However, there are people who specialize in producing footsteps to match movement. They are called Foley editors and are listed in directories of facilities.

Sound formats

Transferring sound from one format to another is less complicated than dealing with archive footage, but, when contacting the source, you must check in what form the sound recording exists. There is equipment to improve the quality of very early or damaged records but, as this does not exist in every recording studio, special arrangements must be made. Possible formats you might encounter include:

- vinyl or shellac discs – 78 rpm, 45 rpm, 33.3 rpm
- compact discs
- laser discs
- reel-to-reel magnetic tape
- cassette audio tapes – analogue or Digital Audio Tape (DAT)
- cartridges (known as 'carts'), which are largely used in radio to play jingles and advertisements.

Editing each presents different problems, depending on the format in which it exists, and this must be built into calculations when booking time. Again, check which alternatives the source holds.

There are other, obsolete methods of sound recording. Before magnetic tape was invented, a system of recording using wire was used. If material is found in this format, it must be transferred to something that can be incorporated into the production. Archives should be able to give advice and arrange transfer of very old or damaged recordings. Damaged material can be repaired electronically, not just by cutting out the click that a scratched disc produces (which leads to some loss of sound), but also by analysing what went before the damaged section and what comes after and restoring the missing part. This works for discs, cylinders, wax discs and the soundtrack on com-opt film.

Sound

Graphics

It is difficult to comprehend statistics and other figures solely through what is said. Therefore, it is usually best done on screen graphically. Using every-day examples to present statistics makes it more comprehensible to a non-specialist audience. People cannot really take in huge figures, so consider ways to bring home to them the full implications, for example what the equiv-alent is for every man, woman and child in the country.

To make your point, you can use:

- words (the names of people or quotations)
- diagrams
- maps
- drawings
- newspaper cuttings.

A programme strand will have a house style and the graphic designer will work to it. You need to summarize the information to be included. Remember to keep it simple, because television screens are small and the monitors in people's homes will not be of such high quality as those used professionally.

Animation – making it move – adds interest and can enhance the message. You can build up information by adding points, and perhaps using sound effects, such as a cash register, to emphasize those points.

Talk to the designer as early as possible. What you want might seem simple, but it may be complicated to realize. Put what you want into writing. It is a good idea to give numbers in words as well as figures to prevent confusion over missed zeros or decimal points. If you are using a map, indicate the loca-tion of places to be marked and decide how large an area will be needed. Do you need to show the whole of a country or just part of it?

Check spellings before giving material to designers (this is your responsi-bility, not theirs) and the finished work too. Everyone makes mistakes when working under pressure.

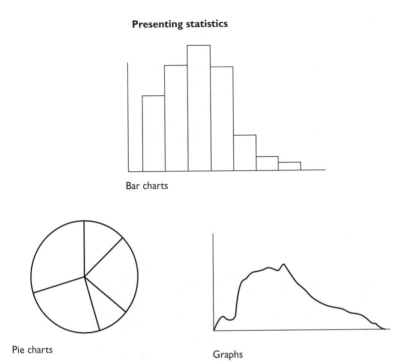

Presenting statistics

Bar charts

Pie charts

Graphs

Presenting statistics

Presenting statistics and figures graphically is largely a technique associated with news and studio-based programmes, so a documentary made on location may have to come up with another method. A pie chart dropped suddenly into a sequence shot in someone's office looks incongruous. You could, for example, suggest recording in a training room where someone is ostensibly explaining facts and figures using visual aids.

As well as bar charts, pie charts and graphs, you can think of more interesting ways to present figures, perhaps using symbols, such as cigarettes for a story on smoking, or men, women and children for an item on computer usage or sweet consumption.

Maps

When using maps, decide if you need to show the whole area as well as a particular region. This is worth considering when talking about a foreign country – the audience's knowledge of geography may be a little shaky.

Any place that is going to be mentioned in the script needs to be shown. If you are talking about a small village that the majority of the audience will not know, put in the nearest large town or city as an indication of the place's location and indicate the major roads between the two.

The use of graphics is not confined to statistics and maps. They can be used for a variety of other purposes, such as credit sequences or special effects. They are produced in two ways:

■ computer generated – this is the usual method and there are a variety of machines and the limits to what can be produced are chiefly time and money
■ drawn – although more rare, this technique can still be considered.

You might want to show an artist's impression of what something looked like, for example an historic building that no longer exists. A mix from actuality to a computer-generated animation is effective, as long as the two match visually in shape and colour.

Props and models

A message may be conveyed better by showing, rather than describing, an object or a process. The simplest props can be obtained by either buying or hiring. If something more complex is needed, such as a representation of the DNA double helix or something to show the inner workings of a machine, a model can be built. The major consideration here is whether the prop or model needs to be what is called 'practical', that is, it works, or whether it is to be used as a dressing prop. If, for example, the production needs a kitchen on set, do the stove and the sink need to work or are they simply to be in the background? Again, time and money have to be considered. If something is being hired from a commercial supplier, it must be specified whether the object is to be practical or not.

If someone will be demonstrating how an object works, there should always be at least one spare. If something can go wrong it will and this applies particularly to props. Presenters and reporters may need to rehearse more than once for a complicated or elaborate process. Continuity is another factor – candles burn down and liquid may be used up, so there must be enough available to ensure that shots will match when cut together.

The safety and insurance aspects of props and models must be taken into account. Fire, smoke, firearms, water, electricity, gas, real money, a very valuable object (e.g. jewellery or a painting), animals and a number of other props will need special arrangements made and you must allow for the cost of these, as well as that of the prop or model. A fireman, a handler or a security guard may need to be in attendance and their fees must be included in the calculations. Enquire whether insurance is included in the hire fee or whether it must be arranged separately. The production's own insurance may cover some props, but not others.

Records of props used must also be kept. In the same way as the records for stills and moving pictures, these records must include where the props came from and what special arrangements need to be made for their use.

Some objects are so precious that their owners will not allow them off-site. Access to a museum or historic house may have to be arranged. If this is going to be a complicated or expensive procedure, check whether a still or moving film of the object already exists and whether obtaining that would be an easier or cheaper option.

Props and models checklist

- How will the objects be obtained? Will it be by buying them, hiring them or commissioning a model?
- Will the object need to be practical (i.e. work) or is it just for dressing?
- What special arrangements need to be made for fire, water, electricity, hazardous substances, flammable objects, glass, firearms and other weapons, smoke guns, food and drink (hygiene), valuable objects (e.g. money or jewellery) and animals? (This list is not exhaustive – think about every object that you use.)
- What insurance will be needed?
- What security arrangements will be needed (e.g. guards or firemen)?
- If the object is going to be used in a demonstration, who will give it and will any special training be needed?

Props and models

Locations

There are many factors to be considered and questions to be asked. Each production will find itself facing different problems. Although no two recordings are ever quite the same, the ability to anticipate and, if possible to forestall, problems is the researcher's most useful skill in this area. Where the recording presents problems, due to time or complexity, expert help should be sought. There are companies, listed in directories of facilities, that specialize in finding locations and it might be more time- and cost-effective to use one, especially when the needs are very specific or unusual. For productions that present no complications, however, researchers will be expected to assess locations.

While collecting information and considering contributors, you should also be thinking about where the recording is to take place. Sometimes this will be dictated by the story or the programme's format, if it is studio-based or done as an outside broadcast.

Your contacts may be able to advise on possible locations. After all, they know more about the subject than you do, so this can save a lot of time. However, they are not programme-makers, so they may not fully understand what you need or any problems that might be associated with recording in particular places.

On location, there is usually an element of choice – a programme about education could be recorded in a number of schools or colleges. As the usual practice is to film experts or authority figures in their office, the automatic assumption is that a headteacher will be filmed in his or her office. However, the story might be given more impact by placing the headteacher in a class-room, a playing field or the lavatories (inside or outside). Even if this is not your decision, you can suggest alternatives, and the reasons for them, to the person responsible.

The recce

For complicated productions or where recording is likely to take place over a long period, you need more information about the location or studio than can be obtained by a simple telephone call or visit. Information can come from:

- people – those on site and those who have used the location before
- documents, such as maps, plans, photographs and general information prepared for previous productions.

However, these are not a substitute for seeing the location. Before you go, get a large-scale map of the area and check for anything that might affect recording, such as airfields, factories and schools. All these might produce noise that will cause delays. People arriving for work or school can also cause traffic problems. You will also need a road map to work out how the production team and crew will get there.

Ideally, the director and cameraman/woman should recce the site, not only to look for the shots that will be needed but also to assess the facilities. If they cannot go, it may be the researcher's job to visit the location and report back.

It is always a good idea to take a second person, perhaps the production assistant or, in certain circumstances, a safety officer as a second pair of eyes. The latter is especially important if the filming is to take place on water, in the air or at great heights or if it will involve stunts.

Notes made about the location should be supplemented with photographs (a Polaroid camera should be enough) or a camcorder. These are useful to allow the director to see potential shots, but notes about the facilities (those things which may not be seen on the end product but are vital to the welfare and safety of crew and contributors) need to be added. You also need to think about where the sun and the shade will be at particular times of day. For example, when will the sun be shining through a particular stained glass window in a church? When will the best effects be achieved? When will a spot be in such deep shade that filming is practically impossible?

If you are recording near a school, it is a good idea to schedule outside shots to avoid those times the children will be arriving or leaving so that they do not interrupt the production. Parents delivering or collecting their children at the school gates will also create problems with transport and parking.

The main practical considerations connected with locations are:

- whether the recording is internal, inside either television/film studios or buildings (e.g. a house or office) or external (i.e. in the open air)
- permissions – who owns the site
- facilities – what exists on site and what will need to be brought in
- contracts – what are the conditions for its use.

Supplement this list with further information, such as parking facilities, hotels, hospitals and places to eat, which will make life easier for you and the rest of the team.

Permissions and licences
Almost everywhere filming takes place will require permission from some person or organization and this may take time to obtain. You will need to find out who owns the site where you hope to work and how long the process takes.

Even if a fee is not being paid, a contract should still be issued for the use of a location to make sure that the production's insurance will cover any accident or damage that may occur. All productions must have insurance against damage to property or injury to the public.

A contract will also protect the production if the person or organization has a change of heart about participating. When the contract is drawn up, try to make sure every eventuality is covered – whose responsibility will security on the site be? Whose responsibility is it to restore the site to its original condition if any changes have to be made?

Filming in the street should be notified to the local police. Although police permission is not legally required, the production can fall foul of a number of laws (e.g. causing a public nuisance and obstruction), so it is advisable to gain the police's co-operation before going out with a crew. Radio is easier – one or two people with a tape recorder and hand-held microphone are unlikely to cause any major problems, unless the recording is being made in sensitive circumstances, such as a riot or public demonstration.

Trespassing on land is another grey area. In Britain, in theory, trespassers can only be taken to court if they cause damage. Trespass is a civil matter, not a criminal one, so it would be the owner of a property who would take any proceedings, although the police can be summoned to help remove intruders.

Minor or major alterations to the location may have to be made. There is usually a clause in any contract where this is necessary to the effect that the place will be restored to its previous condition. Whether the production team is responsible or a company specializing in this kind of work is hired will have to be arranged.

Filming on water

Filming on water, whether inland or at sea, brings in a whole set of separate problems. Permission is usually still needed and special safety equipment, such as life jackets and safety harnesses, should be obtained, even if the crew will be filming from land. The water should also tested, if there is any chance of someone falling in or if someone will intentionally be in the water. There are a whole range of diseases that can be carried in water, as well as pollution hazards.

Tides and currents have to be researched and not only if you will be at sea. You need to check if the stretch of a river you will be working on is tidal. Any boats you hire should have insurance, but this may not cover the production team. Check the terms of the insurance for the boat and its crew.

Filming from the air

Insurance is also a major consideration when filming from the air, which is another potentially dangerous situation. If any complicated filming is to take place, permission must be obtained from the Civil Aviation Authority. There may be restrictions on the route that can be taken and the height at which you can fly.

Recording in a public place

The police need to be informed of any filming and what is involved. If the production is reconstructing something like a robbery, a whole set of complications arise. It does not matter how obvious the film crew is, there will always be a good citizen who alerts the police to what appears to be a crime and there are things that cannot be done in a public place, especially where guns or replica guns are involved.

Streets might need to be closed off for a period (this is where police co-operation is essential) and people other than those being filmed can be inconvenienced. Make sure that everyone is informed and warned of the ways in which they might be affected without overemphasizing the drawbacks. This can vary from putting a note through doors to calling a meeting of local residents if a great deal of co-operation over a long period is required. Try to find out if any roadworks are planned for the time of the recording – the local council should be able to supply this kind of information.

Assessing studios

Considerations about facilities apply to studios as well. In addition to the considerations listed opposite, the following factors need to be taken into account:

- size of the floor space in relation to the set/s
- the number of cameras needed
- lighting rig
- the type of equipment in the gallery
- machines for playing in VT inserts and recording
- seating and facilities for an audience if necessary
- telephone lines or intercom facilities
- health and safety implications of any effects or actions (see pp. 98–99).

Rehearsal rooms

These are obviously used mainly for drama productions but you might be working on a factual programme that involves dramatization and need somewhere to rehearse. If it is to include extensive sequences, there ought to be an experienced drama team, including an AFM/ASM (assistant floor/stage manager), who will sort out the rehearsals themselves, but should you need simply to book a room, you can get advice from the local regional film commission. Most have publications listing facilities and providers of services in their area. The number in the cast will affect the size of the room needed and you will also have to check dates and accessibility, depending on how the cast and production team will be getting there.

Filming overseas

All the matters that apply to filming at home apply to filming abroad, but there are additional factors. The best and most-up-to-date information will come from people who have been working there recently. The country's embassy or high commission will also be able to supply information and advice. It is important to know if a visa is needed and if the regulations are different for any member of the crew from a different country. Ask the embassy about public holidays – there is no point in arriving just at the point the whole country shuts down.

Health considerations

You must also find out what inoculations are needed, not only to work in the country, but also in any country where you might spend time in transit on the way there. It is also worth checking whether there is any local outbreak of a disease. Medication against malaria may need to be started before leaving home and you may also need water purification tablets.

In case of accidents, it is advisable in some countries to take sterile syringes and other first aid supplies for use in hospitals which might not have the proper equipment and where blood-borne diseases such as HIV/AIDS or hepatitis are a danger.

Local conditions

Before you go, it is essential to find out as much as you can about current affairs and local practices to avoid political problems and giving personal offence. Your local university or language school may arrange short courses about living and working in the foreign country to which you are travelling, but if not there are guides on the subject.

It is also worth finding out what the local attitude to alcohol is. Some places are strict about enforcing prohibition, others will tolerate foreigners drinking as long as they are discreet.

You should get a local fixer and translator (in some countries, the government will supply one whether you want one or not), but you really do need a person who speaks the language, understands the law and knows the local conditions and practices. Although you can get an international driving licence, a local driver is advisable in some countries, because there will be enough problems without having to master a whole new set of motoring laws which are very different from those you are used to.

Weather is another important factor. Trying to film during the monsoon season in the Far East is a mission doomed to failure. It is worth finding out what the average temperatures in the day and at night will be, so you know what clothing to take. There are places where the temperature falls significantly at night.

Assessing locations checklist

- Permission.
- Transport and parking – although crews usually make their own way to the location, where parking is difficult it may be better to hire a transit van for everyone. If you are using a studio, how will the contributors and perhaps audience be transported there?
- Accommodation and catering.
- Facilities, such as medical and veterinary, public telephones, garages and toilets. Will anyone involved need special facilities, for example a toilet that can accommodate a wheelchair?
- Power supply – is there electricity on site, how is it produced, will a generator be needed? Remember that other countries may have different electricity supplies.
- Special equipment – standard equipment cannot be used in certain environments, for example in mines or anywhere there is the danger of an explosion or in operating theatres where a sterile atmosphere must be maintained.
- Safety equipment, for example harnesses for working at heights, hard hats and ear defenders, may also be necessary.
- Additional equipment, such as lenses, camera mountings and tracks for moving shots.
- Weather – what is it likely to be and what alternatives are there if the conditions are too bad for outside recording?
- Local events, such as a demonstration or a festival (unless that is what is being filmed).
- Airfields and other noisy industrial and commercial operations.
- Factories, schools, local businesses that might be affected by or disturb filming and whose co-operation you will need.
- Any unusual acoustic effect, such as echos.

Filming overseas

Health and safety

While assessing locations for the shots that are needed and where they are to be recorded, matters of health and safety should be always in your mind. Think about all three while conducting a recce.

Use the list opposite to assess potential hazards (this is why it is a good idea to take a safety officer on a recce, especially to a workplace). After identifying the hazards, think about how likely they are to cause accidents (this is known as risk assessment), especially to people who are not accustomed to the conditions. When you have done this, you can work out ways to prevent problems.

The best way is to remove whatever poses the risks. Often this is not possible so the next step is to find ways to minimize them. This can be by using safety equipment, for example harnesses or protective clothing. Or it could be by marking the hazard with a notice. Or will you need to have someone in place to warn people?

Finally, there must be contingency plans. Check fire exits and, if recording in a large workplace, familiarize yourself with the fire drill arrangements. Decide how to deal with any accident. You need to know if anyone in the crew is a trained first-aider and the location of the nearest hospital with an accident and emergency unit. All accidents must be reported to your employer and the person responsible on site.

Special points to note

- Additional care must be taken when working with children, animals or anyone with a disability that might put them at particular risk. It is no use putting up notices if there are people on site who cannot read them.
- If the production is going to use radio microphones and walkie-talkies at an event which is being recorded for transmission, you may need a licence.
- Safety of property and equipment can include protecting it from theft. If you need to leave equipment anywhere overnight, find out if there is secure storage for it. Also make sure that the demands of recording will not put property on site at risk from thieves or vandals.
- If the recording is to take place where there is a significant risk of fire from even a spark (such as in a mine or at a fireworks factory) you may have to use a clockwork camera and film rather than videotape. This is a specialist skill, so not all camera operators are able to use one.

Health and safety checklist

Hazards include:

- obstacles (cables, stairs, etc.)
- confined spaces
- moving heavy objects (including carrying equipment)
- electricity
- fire
- heat (lamps and heaters)
- water (working on or with water and spills)
- gas and vapours
- chemicals
- heights (falls from a height or objects falling from a height)
- noise
- vehicles and traffic
- aircraft
- hygiene (food and waste)
- weapons
- stunts.

Special care is needed when working with:

- children
- animals
- anyone with a disability (sight, hearing, mobility or inability to read).

Practise safe working by:

1 anticipating hazards
2 minimizing hazards (eliminating them, marking them or warning people about them)
3 taking action in the event of accidents (knowing the fire drill, knowing who is a first aider and knowing where emergency services and hospitals are).

Recording the production

By the time the programme comes to be recorded, either in the studio or on location, the bulk of the research should have been done. There may still be items to check, but at this stage the researcher's role is one of monitoring what is happening to see if any new developments require changes to be made, reacting to circumstances and general dogsbodying so that the recording process goes ahead smoothly. On a live broadcast, however, or when collecting and setting up interviewees on the spot for, perhaps, a vox pop (see p. 70), the role is a more active one.

Checking captions, materials and sources

Before the recording starts, anything that has been obtained from a supplier must be checked against the order to ensure it is as requested, undamaged and in the right condition to be used. Where possible, this should be done in advance, but inevitably there will be situations when something has to be delivered on the day.

In the studio, the spelling of names and organizations must be correct and must be checked on the list of contributors given to the person preparing name captions. Ensure that the list is in the right order. As the programme is going out, make sure that the name on the monitor indicating the next caption is correct. This is usually someone else's responsibility (the studio director or PA), but there is no harm in double-checking, so long as you do it with tact.

On a show using a number of VT inserts, it is usual for a member of the production team to be responsible for ensuring that they come up in the correct order and that any changes made in the running order are monitored and reported to the VT operators.

On location, the director may want to do some simple rostrum camerawork, so check which pictures are needed. Ensure that any props or models have been delivered or will be taken to the location, whether it is you or someone else doing it.

Briefing presenters

When working with reporters or presenters, much will depend on the amount of involvement they have already had with the preparation. They may need to know:

- the background to the story
- the structure of the programme and where the sequence they are recording fits in
- the running order or schedule for the recording
- why and how the contributors they are interviewing are being used
- any particular questions to ask and any special information relating to contributors, including what not to ask.

Presenters and other members of the production team will also need to be informed of any changes that affect them, such as alterations to the shooting schedule or to the running order.

Looking after contributors

It is not enough to make sure that contributors turn up in the right place at the right time. They must also be in the right frame to mind to give their best, including being sober. Contributors need to be well briefed about what is wanted from them so that they feel confident, but not to the point of rehearsing their replies. Many will want to do this while equipment is being set up, but they need to be tactfully steered away from it because the end result will be dull and flat. They may also find the process of being wired up with a microphone uncomfortable. Where you can, introduce contributors to the crew, as this will help them feel less strange. As well as making them at much at their ease as possible, their safety must be considered. Think about the following.

- Equipment – the crew is used to taking action to avoid hazards, but the contributors will not be. Ensure that they do not trip over wires or collide with pieces of equipment. In the event of an emergency, contributors must be escorted to safety.
- Environment – on location, weather conditions may have made the ground difficult to walk on. High winds can present problems and strong sunlight can dazzle.
- Action – what are contributors required to do? Will the demands of filming add hazards to carrying out an action, even if it is something they do all the time, e.g. a cook in a restaurant kitchen?

During the period when the equipment is being set up, or during any other delay, contributors who are not used to the media can become very tense. You can help to minimize this problem by talking to them. If the contributors require make-up, ensure that the person responsible for summoning them to the studio knows where they are and that the make-up person knows at what time they will be needed.

Working with animals

Although everyone warns against working with animals, it is sometimes unavoidable. There are legal regulations for the use of wild and domestic animals (see pp. 132–3). Although animals hired should have competent handlers, this cannot always be applied to pet owners. 'He's only playing . . .' is a phrase which often precedes a nasty situation. You may also find that other contributors on the show, especially children, are terrified of animals or birds. They may also have an allergy.

Working with children

Although children must have a competent adult to escort them, either a parent or a chaperone, their curiosity about anything new (particularly equipment) needs to be borne in mind. Like pet owners, some parents can be over-tolerant of their offspring's quirks, which can lead to accidents. There are stringent restrictions covering children who have to give a performance. You will need to get permission from parents or guardians even for documentary programmes. There are restrictions on what children may be asked to do and the number of hours they can work, as shown on this chart:

AGE	MAX. HRS ON LOCATION/ IN STUDIO	PERMITTED TIMES OF DAY ON SITE	MAX. LENGTH OF CONTINUOUS PERFORMANCE	MAX. LENGTH OF TOTAL HRS OF PERFORMANCE/ REHEARSAL
Under 2 yrs	3	0930–1600	20 mins	1
2–5	5	0930–1630	30 mins	2
5–9	7.5	0900–1700	45 mins	3
13–16	8	0900–1900 or 1000–2000*	1 hr	3.5

Notes:
A child is legally defined as someone who is under the school leaving age. Employing children as performers is covered by the Children (Performances) Regulations (1968).
There are also minimum intervals for meals and rest. There are restrictions on the type of performances children under 14 may give and they must be licensed by the Chief Magistrate at Bow Street Court, 192 Bow Street, London WC2 7AS. All children under the age of 18 must be licensed to perform outside the United Kingdom and the Irish Republic.
* This only applies to studio performances, and a licence must be obtained.

Dealing with the public

Filming usually attracts a crowd, often containing noisy children. Sometimes an appeal to their better natures and an explanation of what is happening will keep them quiet. In term time, you can also ask why they are not in school or threaten them with the police. Children are not the only ones who can be difficult. When you are recording in a public place (e.g. a park), there are always people with someone they ought not to be with. They can be very difficult if they realize their indiscretions may appear before millions of people. Consider taking along extra help to deal with the public.

Monitoring interviews

Once the contributor is in front of the camera, your responsibilities are not over. Although whoever is asking the questions will be aware of the content of the replies, he or she usually has other things to consider. A studio presenter may also be getting instructions through an earpiece about timing, the next question to ask and other matters not directly concerned with the exact detail of what the interviewee is saying. It is easy for a contributor to make a mistake, either by getting a fact wrong or, more seriously, by contravening the law (perhaps expressing an opinion which might be construed as defamation). Although it is usually possible to correct mistakes during editing, it is obviously better to remedy any errors on the spot. If the programme is being transmitted live, it is not possible to edit, so monitoring interviews is particularly important.

When working on location with a single-camera crew, you might have to note the questions being asked so that, after the interviewee's answer has been recorded, reversal shots of the interviewer asking those questions can be taken, allowing the interview to be edited. This needs to be done accurately because the question must lead into the reply actually given.

Continuity

Continuity is the process of noting what happens in one shot so that there are no unexplained changes in the action or dress of the participants from one shot to another when the footage is edited together. For anything other than the simplest shoot, there should be someone to take continuity notes, either a production assistant or, for really complicated recordings, a continuity assistant. If there is no such person, you should be prepared to make notes that will ensure that the recording will edit together smoothly.

Polaroid cameras are useful to back up notes and diagrams on the following.

- Dress (e.g. on which lapel is a brooch being worn or on which side a shoulder bag or briefcase is being carried). If the filming is taking place over more than one day, the clothes being worn should be listed (ties and earrings can be a problem). Contributors must wear the same outfit on different filming days if necessary.
- Action – which hand is a person using to hold an object or open a door? Are people walking left to right or right to left?
- The set – where is the furniture, what is on a table or a mantelpiece? This is particularly important if objects are going to be moved or you will be returning to the same place later on.

Before you go

If you are recording on location, it is good public relations to tidy up before you leave, especially if you are using someone's home. Offer to wash up or dispose of polystyrene cups and other litter. Put the furniture back if it has been re-arranged and check that no damage has been caused (if it has, reassure the owner about insurance).

Logging rushes

As it is expensive to hire edit suites, a lot of preparation needs to take place before the final edit. A list of shots needs to be made so that the director can make a rough list of how she or he wants to put together the final item or programme. This is called a 'paper edit'. To do this quickly and efficiently, the director must know where the shots needed are on the tape(s) so someone, e.g. the PA, researcher, video journalist or director, needs to view the rushes (the unedited footage) and at the same time log the time-code and details of the shots. It is not worth including unsuccessful shots, as this just wastes time. You do not always need to include frame numbers as just minutes and seconds is usually enough. However, sometimes, if you are logging a number of tapes, hours might be necessary.

The shot-list includes a brief description of each shot with the shot size and content. If speech is included, you need to give the opening and closing words of what was said. This enables the director to get a mental picture of how the footage will cut together, so if people are walking in and out of shot, you need to include the direction in which they were moving.

A short and simple sequence can then be done in the edit suite from a paper-edit but for a complete programme, a pre-edit may be done off-line (see p. 108).

If you are doing the editing, turn up at the suite with all the tapes you need, the paper edit assembly and any other paperwork or additional material (e.g. discs). Try to organize your (expensive) time there, so that it is fully utilized. If you have to be elsewhere for some of the time, plan things so that the editor can get on with something that does not need your presence, such as cutting a sequence to music.

Time-code

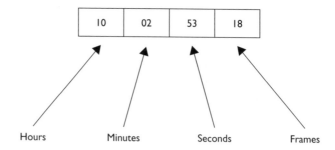

| 10 | 02 | 53 | 18 |

Hours   Minutes   Seconds   Frames

An example

TIME	SHOT	DURATION
	Interview with Tom Lewis (instructor)	
00.20	'We set up this course . . .	
03.02	. . . more resources.'	2'42"
03.06	Reverses Amanda	
03.57	'People might say you're rewarding bad behaviour.	
	What do you say to that?'	4"
	Vox pops	
04.17	'Cos you learn something useful.'	2"
04.49	'I never used to go to school . . .	
05.19	. . . but they treat you like an adult.'	15"
05.39	'It's better than sitting at home . . .	
06.52	. . . I can get a job.'	13"
07.20	'Cos they said they'd stop my benefits.'	2"
07.44	GVs workshop	
09.11	CU welding gun	
09.19	CU tyres	
10.58	CU car engine	
12.01	WS Tom talking to trainees about safety	
15.32	Trainee rolling tyre R to L	9"
16.41	Trainee rolling tyre L to R	11"
17.09	2-S trainees changing tyre	13"
18.56	GVs of training centre (external)	
	PTC Amanda intro	
21.41	'Getting young people into training is . . .	
22.04	. . . a new approach.'	23"

Shot sizes

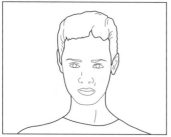

MCU (Medium Close Up) is the standard head-and-shoulders shot

CU (Close Up) shows the face from the base of the neck to the top of the head.
It is mainly used in drama or for an emotional or very important moment.

MS (Mid Shot) extends down to the waist

LS (Long Shot) shows the whole figure

WS (Wide Shot) shows the setting

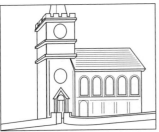
GV (General View) shows the location

2-S (2 Shot) shows two people

3-S (3 Shot) shows three people

OS (Over the Shoulder) is mainly used in documentaries for interviews and shows the interviewer's shoulder in the foreground

POV (Point of View) is used for effects, e.g. showing a dog's eye view of the world

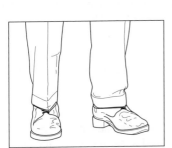

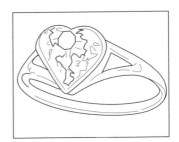
BCU (Big Close Up) shows the face from chin to hairline and is mainly used for moments of high drama or very close detail of an object

The editing process

Off-line editing

This means keeping a master copy of the recorded footage (including any archive material), whether on film or video, and making a second copy on a cheaper, less high quality format. Both have time-code. The cheaper version has this in vision and will be edited in an off-line suite, which has fewer facilities and is less expensive than the on-line suite where the final version will be put together.

Once the off-line edit has been done, a list of the time-codes on the shots used is made which can then be repeated, or conformed, using the master copy at an on-line edit. Any special effects are added at this point, so notes of those needed must also be made during the off-line edit.

Linear editing

Editing can be done using either a linear or a non-linear system. Linear editing, as the name suggests, has to start at the beginning and go on to the end. It is not possible to change a sequence when reviewing the whole production at the end. The choices then are either:

- to use the existing tape as a source tape, cut out or add other material and go down a generation, which will involve loss of quality or
- to relay the whole thing up to or after the section to be changed, which is time-consuming.

These disadvantages mean that linear editing is best used either to make a final master or for simple news-type items.

Non-linear editing

Non-linear editing restores the flexibility of film to video editing. The master version (either on film or video) of the production is transferred to a computer disc, again with time-code, to ensure accurate matching. As the material is on disc, it can be accessed in any order. It is also possible to store two or three versions of an edited sequence to decide which one to use. A list of time-codes is produced and the master version conformed. Non-linear editing systems can also do effects and these can be incorporated into the final list.

Apart from the material actually being edited, commentary, captions, music and sound effects are usually put on at this stage. Everything needed must be written or selected before going to the edit. Music must be brought along or delivered in the right format. This will involve checking in advance that the facilities to cope with any unusual formats are available or that transfer from one format to another has been arranged. Most facilities have a full set of sound effects, but it is worth checking they have the one you need if it is unusual.

After editing

Once the edit is finished, there will be documentation to be arranged. This will fall into one of the following.

■ Technical information needed for transmission – the format the production is on, the length of the complete programme or item, the length and nature of opening and end credit sequences, any extended periods of silence, unusual colour effects, etc.
■ Additional information that the commissioner might need for presentation announcements, such as the date when the programme was recorded, if this is significant, or what happened to major participants after recording. There may be other material, such as fact sheets or publications for sale connected to the programme. You must also consider what additional information about the programme needs to be passed to the company broadcasting it so it can answer viewers' and listeners' queries. Names, addresses of organizations, locations, sources of any quoted material and music should be listed.

It is not just factual information that viewers want. If the programme contains potentially contentious material, the broadcasting company will also need to be alerted so they can take the decision whether to make an announcement before transmitting it.

Even if the production is not intended for broadcasting (e.g. a corporate or training video), there may be additional information that the client will need, which should be checked.

The editing process

The script

Audio-visual productions consist of a combination of words and pictures, which work together. The script should add to what the viewer can see. It is like showing a series of pictures to a friend, putting them into context and drawing attention to the most important part.

The commentary on a factual production should be almost the last stage of programme-making. Televised news programmes, being produced to a tighter deadline, will have a more detailed preliminary script, but it will not be finalized until the pictures are edited. If the pictures are cut to fit the words, the end result is either radio with pictures or an illustrated lecture. This does not mean that nothing can be done before the editing and dubbing stages. There will often be a rough outline of the script before recording starts and during the course of the production, notes of phrases and sentences that could be used are made.

Be careful here that you do not break the copyright laws. When you make your notes, remember to include the source of any material and whether you have quoted directly or summarized what another person has said or written. It is a good idea to put any direct copying of information from another source, such as a book, in quotation marks with the page number in brackets.

Writing words to pictures is a fine art. What the viewer is seeing and hearing must be connected. If they are not connected, it is the picture that is remembered rather than the words. The commentary must not simply describe what is being shown, it must add information that tells the audience more. Although what the viewer will see can be slightly anticipated, referring back will not work as the moment – and the picture – have passed.

Timing the script

A rough estimate can be made by calculating three words per second, but people vary in their speaking speed and the language and punctuation used may also affect the timing. As it is not necessary, indeed it is often more effective, not to write over every shot, the length of any silences have to be timed accurately. Time the script by counting the words (some computer programs will allow you to do this). If you read it yourself and use a stopwatch, you will not get an accurate result, unless you are experienced in doing voice-overs.

Working with writers

In television or radio, the writer is usually someone involved in the preparation of the story – the producer, presenter or reporter. The writer of the script or commentary of a non-broadcast video, however, might not be involved until the later stages. At whatever stage the writer joins the production, he or she may need notes of relevant research, briefing on the nature of the programme and the audience at which it is aimed, and copies of the visual material to be included. The writer must also know about any legal or ethical issues.

Corporate videos and training tapes have additional considerations. Specialist writers are usually brought in and most expect to do their own research.

Here, it is important to remember that these productions will usually be seen again and again over a long period of time. What changes will there be?

The researcher's role is to check the script for factual accuracy and to make suggestions to make it more comprehensible to the audience. If you are asked to prepare or contribute to a draft script yourself, consider the following factors.

Language

The language used should be appropriate to the intended audience. Programmes that are aimed at a specialized sector can afford to use more slang or jargon. However, in general, it is best avoided because slang and jargon date, which will limit future sales; and they exclude those who do not understand them, which will limit the audience.

Simple words can be more powerful and direct than long, complicated ones. Compare 'The child's mother said they did not know about the danger' and 'The maternal parent of the infant declared neither was informed of the perilous circumstances'. Which is easier to understand and has the greater sense of immediacy?

Verbs give impetus. Did someone run, jog, trot, escape, flee or bolt rather than 'go'? Active verbs convey urgency and vigour, so they should used in preference to the passive tense, although this can be a useful technique to avoid pinning responsibility or blame on someone who might sue.

If the phrase seems comfortingly familiar, ask yourself if it is a cliché. Sometimes news and current affairs programmes use them as a kind of shorthand – the viewer or listener understands in broad terms what is meant and that is probably enough for a news bulletin. Journalists are up against much shorter deadlines than other programme-makers, so such short cuts are sometimes necessary but, if you have more time, try for a less obvious phrase.

Grammar

Among the audience will be people who were educated in the days when the rules of grammar were considered to be much less flexible than they are now.

As a result of their nuisance value, experts on grammar can take up an irritating amount of your or someone else's time replying to both letters and telephone calls. Therefore, it is simpler all round not to break the better known rules.

Areas of contention include the script using 'he' to refer to both men and women, and if words that are deemed offensive are used for those from a particular ethnic origin or for someone with a specific physical or mental condition. If someone says 'The Queen of England' offended Scots will get in touch to point out that she is sovereign of Britain. Again, the hassle is not worth it.

Meaning

A UK radio station used to run hourly forecasts introduced as 'the weather brought to you by Kuoni Travel'. This was wrong as it is God or meteorological forces that cause the weather. The travel company was bringing the weather *forecast*. Many listeners are intelligent enough to be so irritated by this that they miss the next few seconds. Quantum describes the smallest amount of radiant energy and a quantum jump is a small, but significant, advance. Enough of the population has a scientific background to consider that anyone who uses 'quantum leap' to imply a large change is not to be trusted in other areas.

Check whether there are any dangling participles, a phrase at the beginning of the sentence which does not refer to the subject of it (e.g. 'Getting into a taxi this week, the driver spotted my clerical attire' – it was the cleric who was climbing into the taxi, not the driver). Sentences like this can cause unease in the listener and will distract attention from what is being said for a moment.

Juxtaposition

This happens when material is written in a hurry. The sentence beginning 'The poet who survived the war with his family in Sarajevo' was said to introduce a news item. The context in this example made it clear that it was the civil war in former Yugoslavia to which the reporter referred, not a family feud. Although vocal inflections and timing may make it clearer what was intended, there is still a hiatus in which the listener mentally adjusts what was heard to what was meant.

Tautology

This is difficult to spot immediately, but makes the script seem flabby. As all school children are young, saying 'a young schoolchild' is saying the same thing twice. Saying someone is a professional surgeon suggests a comparison with an amateur surgeon – someone who carries out brain surgery in the kitchen as a hobby. Ask yourself, do they or would they come any other way?

Redundancy

Some words are unnecessary, as in 'Appropriate measures will be taken'. Ask yourself, what would be the alternative? Inappropriate measures might indeed be taken, but surely not intentionally. The word 'appropriate' is not necessary. This kind of flaccidity is common in written statements from government departments or companies. If you are quoting a statement then what was said, however badly written, must be reported, but there is no need to allow such verbal infelicities to appear in something over which you have some control.

Ambiguity

Check the script for factual accuracy, for any legal implications and for ambiguity. Does the context make it clear that two hundred pounds in weight or two hundred pounds in value is intended? It may be clear on the page, or after a moment's thought, but not when spoken.

Trade names

Many trade names are used as a generic term (e.g. Biro). They should not be used as the general word. This is particularly important if you are comparing a number of similar objects for a consumer programme. You cannot say you will compare 'six kinds of Biro', when you mean ballpoint pens made by different manufacturers. Your programme will be in trouble if it criticizes something erroneously described by a trade name when a rival manufacturer's product is under discussion.

Negative checks

This is the process by which a check is made to ensure that people or organizations are not unintentionally defamed. It applies mainly to drama, but In current affairs or documentary programmes, it is worth checking that no organization of a similar sounding name is operating in the same town so that the script can be absolutely precise about which trading company is exploiting the public in one way or another.

The script

Scripts for studio productions and commentaries

Scripts for studio-based productions are written in advance and a copy of the final version given to the teleprompt operator, but they must be prepared so they relate to the pictures. The script here is usually concerned with conveying factual information, not creating a mood, reflecting an environment or representing a point of view, which a commentary might do. In a magazine programme or a news programme, items are generally introduced by a presenter or newsreader directly to camera. There may be cutaways to stills or clips of footage while the script continues. Hitting the right point in the script will be the responsibility of the director and vision mixer.

Although there will be small variations between the way different companies and productions lay out their scripts and present information, the generally agreed conventions for a television studio script, whether for a live or pre-recorded production, are as follows.

- What is seen appears on the left-hand side of the page, what is heard on the right.
- Visual sources (e.g. camera and VT) appear on the left with each shot numbered. Cut lines indicating where the shots change are marked in the script.
- Any special sound sources (e.g. sound on tape or SOT, which means sync sound, and grams) appear on the extreme right.
- Information for the PA, director or vision mixer appear, often in a square, on the right. They will add timing and any other information they need by hand at the rehearsal.

Studio script layout

2. CAM 1 MCU Presenter	/PRESENTER: Hullo. In today's programme, we'll be talking to someone who says he can communicate with bees,
PAN DOWN TO VEG	looking at ways of cooking some of the exotic vegetables that are appearing in our supermarkets and getting an exclusive interview with the star of a film opening this
3. VT 3 Love Among the Ruins	week/
CAPGEN @ 5"	In: 'Is this seat taken? . . .' Out: '. . . and I never want to see you again.'
Love Among the Ruins Moonlight Productions	Dur: 36"
4. CAM 1 MCU Presenter	/PRESENTER: We'll find out later if that's how it ends. My first guest is someone whose voice is more famous than her face. Nearly a quarter of us wake up to her Breakfast Show on radio but now, she's moving into television to present a series on the changing
5. CAM 2 MCU MARY	role of women./ Mary Meredith, why are you leaving radio?

Writing commentary and voice-overs

In television, the pictures are what the viewer remembers, not the words, so never write the final script before the sequence is edited. You should make notes of useful phrases while doing the research but beware of breaching copyright. With video, there is a temptation to sit in the edit suite, writing the script as you look at the pictures. The result usually just describes the pictures, so it is dull. Make a shot list with the timings and then be brave – go away and write the script. Analyse the cut pictures in sequences, not just in shots, and draft what you need to say in order to make a coherent pattern of the whole piece.

- Think about the audience, their age, background and level of likely knowledge. Although a script or commentary is written, it is intended to be heard. Whatever the purpose, the idea is to produce something that sounds natural when spoken.
- Use facts sparingly. With print, you can go back and re-read complex information, but a viewer cannot. Delay information to retain interest. You can anticipate, but do not refer back to something that has passed. Leave something for the end.
- Do not write over the first and last two seconds – the audience needs time to get into the film and to reflect on what they have seen. Let the pictures speak for themselves – silence is often more powerful than words. Decide when you *need* to say something.
- Use the commentary to give the audience additional information or draw their attention to one aspect of the shot, guiding them to what you want them to notice.
- Do not always finish a sentence at the end of a shot, write in sequences to lead the audience through the whole film. Vary the length and structure of sentences.

Delaying information is a good tactic generally. Although the rule in programme-making is first tell them what you are going to tell them, then tell them, and finally tell them what you have told them, this does not mean that everything has to be revealed immediately. How long you can delay the revelation depends on the audience – how keen will they be to find out, how long will they wait?

Commentary scripts that are going to be pre-recorded need less information than studio scripts, but the spoken words still appear on the right-hand side of the page. Timings are put in on the left.

Commentary script

0.05   John was born in this house seventy-five years ago and has lived
       here all his life. But now his house and those of his neighbours are
       under threat. The whole street is going to disappear because of
       redevelopment.
0.42   It is not only John who's unhappy with how he's been treated.

After writing

Go back to the pictures and check the commentary against them. Read it
aloud. Does it sound the kind of thing you would say to explain what is going
on to another person sitting next to you on the sofa?

Revise the commentary. Can you say it in fewer words? Do you need to
say it? Look for simpler ways of saying it, for clichés, redundancy and tautology
(see pp. 112–113).

Get whoever is reading the commentary to try it out and re-phrase it if necessary to suit their own speech pattern. Does this affect the relationship between
words and pictures or the timing?

Mark up a script with timings for the dub.

Writing questions, intros and links

You may be asked to suggest questions for an interview. Although presenters usually prefer to use their own words, they must be clear why the question is being asked and what information is being elicited. You may also need to warn the presenter of potentially sensitive areas, either because they are to be avoided or because any questions need to be phrased carefully. Any legal issues must also be drawn to the presenter's attention.

Preparing questions for an interview on camera is different from getting ready for a research interview (see pp. 58–59). When information is being gathered before the filming starts, interviews can be a more leisurely and discursive process because at this stage it will often not yet be known what is to be included and how the person is to be used. Questions at this point are designed to gather as much information as possible so that particular opinions or experiences of the potential interviewee can be selected.

When recording or for a live transmission, however, the replies need to be brief. Thus, closed questions are used more often in order to get a concise answer. The research done before recording will have shown which replies the programme will need. You can suggest the kind of question to be asked on camera or you may be asking them yourself. Try to ask the question so that the contributor will answer with a complete sentence. This will make editing easier, especially if the questions are to be cut out from the final interview.

Open questions are still useful, but may be used to elicit a succinct reply by putting in more detail than at the preliminary research stage. For example: 'Tell me about the time when you . . .', 'Tell me what happened after you . . .', 'You have been widely quoted as saying . . .' and 'What is your opinion of this now?'

Sometimes you will want a one-word answer, as when doing a vox pop (see pp. 70–71). The question to be asked should then be phrased to get a short reply. This usually means a closed question, 'Do you think . . .', 'Is the Prime Minister doing the right thing?' or a similar wording.

Intros

Introductions need to prepare the audience for what is to follow, to give them an idea of what to expect so they know why they should be interested. News and magazine programmes often start off with what is called a menu (a list of the major stories or features that will be covered in the programme) to encourage the audience not to turn off or to another channel or station. Here a brief summary of the most important feature of the item and why the audience should be interested is needed. Make sure that all the items mentioned will be appearing. If there is any doubt, do not include it.

Individual items also need an introduction. If it is to lead into a recorded insert, make sure that the last words of the introduction fit the opening of the insert, whether it is spoken or silent. Does the audience need any information to make sense of the item or to put it into context? It may need to be explained when an insert was recorded or why the place where it was done is important.

If it is to introduce a guest, remember that the camera will cut to the guest when his or her name is mentioned. Your description of the guest's achievements should cover the areas of questioning in the interview or the audience's expectations will be raised but not satisfied. Unless there is a good reason not to, delay giving the name until very close to the end, or the camera will stay on the guest for an uncomfortably long time. You will also, of course, build up the suspense – who *is* this person?

Links

These are the short sections of script between items in a programme. They are intended to signal that the previous piece has ended and to introduce the next. Some programmes aim for a connection between the two – perhaps finding a common element, such as 'That was John Smith in Johannesburg. And now, we're going from South Africa to Southend, where a new initiative to revive the tourist trade is being launched today.'

Problems arise when the programme is going from a distressing story to a more upbeat one or vice versa. It is easy to offend listeners and viewers by a facile and apparently heartless link. In these cases, it is better simply to close one story with an 'outro', pause and introduce the next without linking them.

Writing support material

Billings and production information
You may find yourself involved in the preparation of material for the press and public under the following headings.

- Billings – the information included in listings intended for the compilers of the programme pages in newspapers and periodicals. The programme needs to be summed up in one or two sentences to sell it to the viewer, with a further paragraph or two which might be included, depending on the space available.
- Programme information – a summary of the programme's contents and names and addresses of people and organizations.
- Fact sheets need to contain a list of organizations included in the programme with, if necessary, descriptions of the organizations' activities. Sometimes information about related organizations and material which was not used or a more detailed account of, for example, the laws relating to a particular issue will be added.
- Programme summaries and additional information for teletext pages and websites.
- Books and pamphlets connected to the programme which are for sale – material similar to the above, as well as books consulted, stills (some of which may have to be specially supplied and cleared for inclusion) and graphic material.
- Notes for trainers or teachers relating to an educational production.

Back-up material
Many programmes, particularly factual and educational ones, provide support material to viewers or teachers and the researcher may have to provide information for its preparation or write it. This means keeping good records of the programme's contents and of additional information that could be of use, but which might not have been included in the programme. Some of this information might also be used on the teletext pages or on websites. If the programme is to be subtitled, a transcript may be supplied (although this is not always possible) and should be checked for accuracy, particularly in the spelling of names and organizations which might not be clear from the spoken word.

There may be a house style for support publications if the programme is to be part of a series. In this case, material must be prepared to match the layout and style. If, however, there is no set format, decisions about design, layout and writing style have to be agreed with both the members of the production team responsible and the publisher. As in every other area, time and budget will affect the final result. Although the publisher will ultimately be responsible for the look of printed material, the accuracy of the content is down to you, so drafts and the final copy must be meticulously proofread.

Publicity

Drawing attention to the programme is a vital part of the production process. After the programme is made, or even while it is in progress, ways of publicizing it have to be considered. Think about what is to be included – how much of the content should be revealed, what problems are likely to arise, which contributors can be suggested to the press for back-up interviews and which need their identity and privacy protected?

The broadcasting company will also have a department producing its own press material and will need information for publicity purposes. If the production is doing it itself, someone must compile a list of newspapers (national and local) and periodicals (mass market, trade and hobby) intended to attract editorial coverage to whom you can send press releases. If the production is targeted to attract an audience with a particular interest, consider approaching specialist publications. Given the length of time between a journal going to press and its publication, this is not always an option. (Find out their press dates, as they may be put together up to a couple of months in advance, and you will need to allow for this when sending material or talking to the editorial staff.)

All material released to the press and public must be checked for factual accuracy, for any legal implications, including copyright, and for the effect it may have on organizations and individuals. There are occasions when people appearing in a programme must be protected from press attention.

If the production is expected to receive a lot of coverage, because of its subject-matter, you might pass the names of people who are either in the programme or who were considered but not used to print journalists who will write articles. Anyone whose name is given must be told in advance and allowed to decide whether to co-operate. There is a fine balance to be struck between getting publicity and giving away so much information that the audience will think they have read all they need to know about the subject before the programme's transmission.

The broadcasting company might also want stills or clips to use in making trails and making on-air announcements about forthcoming programmes. These need to be selected with equal care.

Writing support material

Appendix A: Copyright

Copyright and other areas of the law are highly specialized areas which change, both because of new Acts and also because of precedents set in test cases. The first modern copyright law was passed in 1911, but it has been modified by legislation in 1956, 1988 and 1995 and further amendments are due. The researcher cannot be expected to know the fine detail of these Acts, but must be aware of their existence.

Copyright is an area in which whole armies of lawyers make a good and regular living. This section cannot transform you into an expert and you should not rely on it because it is necessarily over-simplified – there are exceptions to almost every principle cited here. It also covers the law in the UK, which incorporates some international law; however, you need to check the position not only in your own country but in any country where your production is going to be sold.

Further problems arise with what are often referred to as 'layers of copyright'. You might want to include in your programme a clip of a poet reading from his or her work with a musical background. There may be copyright in the recording, in the poem and in the music to be cleared as well as possible residual fees to the poet for the performance.

This section is just intended as a basic checklist. The books in the reading list will give more information. If you know in advance the kind of problems you are likely to encounter, you will have more time to check the position with an expert and start negotiations.

What is copyright?
Copyright is a form of property, like a building. If you want to use it, you must come to an arrangement with the owner. It can give be given as a gift or left in a will, sold outright to do what you want with or it can be loaned for a fixed time and under agreed conditions, in other words you can rent the whole or part of a building and a certain sum of money may be charged for doing so. Conditions about what use you make of it may also be imposed – whether you can alter it in any way, for example.

This is how copyright works, except that what is owned is the work done, which is sometimes called 'intellectual property'. This might be something written, or a painting, a photograph, a sculpture, a design, a musical composition or a piece of computer software. Rights may also be owned to a film, a tape, a translation of a literary work or the choreography of a ballet. Different rights (e.g. publication or theatric) can be assigned or sold to different people or organizations. Rights can also be bequeathed in a will.

Copyright holders and owners
The person who owns a work is probably not the copyright holder. The copyright holder is the person who created it. So a person who owns a letter does not own the copyright – that belongs to the person who wrote the letter. The owner may charge you for access to the object, but you will also need to get

the copyright owner's permission before you can use it in your production. The British Film Institute libraries, for example, contain both archive film and still pictures, but they do not own the copyright to most of them.

Alternatively, you may pay an art gallery a fee to film in it. This does not cover filming the exhibits – the gallery is unlikely to own the copyright of the works. What you have paid is a facility fee and copyright still has to be negotiated with the artist or sculptor or the owner of the rights, if you are featuring the works. If you use a transparency of a work of art owned by a gallery, you will probably have to pay a reproduction fee, even if the work itself is long out of copyright, because the photograph made of the work is itself copyright.

Is it copyright?

Some of the fees due to people whose work you want to use are not, strictly speaking, to do with copyright. If you want to show an excerpt from a film or television play, certain people (e.g. actors, directors and stunt arrangers) may be due residual payments for repeats agreed in the contract they signed with the company that made the film. These will vary from production to production and original contracts have to be checked. However, performers' rights under the Copyright, Design and Patents Act 1988 often parallel the copyright provisions.

You may also find that if you are filming a band or a group, the musicians will ask for payment. This is not to do with copyright, rather with Musicians Union agreements and you will almost certainly still have to pay the owner of the copyright to the music played.

In general, employees of a company do not own the copyright in work they have done as part of their work, but this will depend on their contract of employment.

The copyright period

From 1 January 1996, copyright in a work in the UK generally lasts for 70 years from the end of the year in which the creator of the work dies. Before that date, the period was 50 years (as it still is in some other countries). Thus, if an author, painter or photographer dies on 1 January, it is 364 days (or 365 days in a leap year) and 70 years before his or her works enter the public domain in the UK and the rest of the European Community.

This period of 70 years applies to all works, from something done while the originator was an infant prodigy aged 5 to the last work published a few days before his or her death. The sole exception to this is *Peter Pan* by J.M. Barrie (d. 1937). He gave the copyright in this work to Great Ormond Street Hospital, which will continue to be able to collect royalties on it, in whatever form it appears, forever. His other works, however, fall within the usual laws of copyright.

If the work is a collaboration, the copyright period extends until 70 years after the death of the longest-lived of the creators. Lennon–McCartney songs, for example, will come out of copyright after those songs that John Lennon wrote alone.

As rights can be divided, you will almost certainly find that if your programme is to be sold abroad, some elements will have to be cleared again with the owner of the copyright in area of the world to which you are selling it. This is particularly likely if your programme is a co-production and contains commercial music or film clips. You may also find that the period of copyright protection is different abroad.

If a production is to be sold on video instead of, or as well as, broadcast, those rights must be cleared with copyright holders too. The amount paid will depend on the size of the potential market, namely is it only likely to be sold to educational establishments or is it being aimed at a mass market?

Revived copyright arrangements
A work that was in copyright on 31 December 1995 simply had its copyright period extended to 70 years. The mathematically or legally minded will realize, however, that the work of a number of authors, such as Rudyard Kipling (d. 1936), and composers, such as Sir Edward Elgar (d. 1934), whose copyright had lapsed, is now back in the copyright period. Whoever owned the copyright before it expired is the owner of this revived copyright. Material which falls into this category can be used without permission, but the copyright holder must be given notice and the terms for its use must be 'reasonable', which is where legal advice may be needed. Work commissioned before 1 July 1995 incorporating material that was then in the public domain but is now back in copyright, is exempt. Proof, like a contract, is required.

The Internet
At the end of 1996, 160 countries agreed treaties on copyright for certain types of work on the Internet. It is far too early to assess all the implications of this for broadcasters, but this is an area that production staff need to be aware of and to review regularly as cases come before the courts and precedents are set.

Work made available posthumously
A work found among an author's papers after his or her death, or discovered many years after, will be in copyright until 50 years after the end of the year in which it was first made available to the public or the year 2040, whichever is the sooner. There are six definitions of how a piece of work might be 'made available to the public'.

The publication right
This is a new area of copyright created by the 1995 Duration of Copyright and Rights in Performance Regulations. Copyright is usually owned by the author of a work but this gives rights to any person or organization that makes available any piece of previously unpublished work in which copyright did exist, but has now expired. The period of copyright under this lasts 25 years.

Parliamentary copyright
Parliament (both Houses) owns the rights to work done by or under its control and copyright is administered either by the Speaker of the House of Commons or by the Clerk of the Parliaments. Parliamentary copyright lasts for

50 years from the end of the calendar year in which the work was made. Various provisions apply to the broadcasting of speeches made in Parliament.

Crown copyright

This applies to work done by servants or employees of the Crown or government as part of their duties. It is a complex area, requiring expert knowledge, as copyright here may be for 125 years, 75 years or 50 years from the end of the calendar year of its making or publication. Note that Acts of Parliament become Crown copyright once Royal Assent has been received.

Anonymous and traditional works

Copyright does exist in anonymous or traditional works, but here the important factor is when and how they were first made available to the public. It is also necessary to investigate very carefully if the work truly is anonymous. Just because no-one in the office knows who did it, does not mean it cannot be discovered (think, for example, of an anonymous novel). You will have to prove that you did all you could to find the copyright owner. Traditional is another area requiring caution. Just because a song is being sung by a folksinger, does not mean it is out of copyright. It may have been specially composed to sound like a folk song.

What can be copyright?

For the purposes of broadcasting and non-broadcast video, it is worth thinking of the kinds of copyright issues that might arise under four categories:

- words
- pictures
- sound
- moral.

Words

Published words can be prose or verse. Are you quoting from a work still in copyright? Is what you are quoting a translation? When was the translation that you are planning to use made? The play you want to do may be a Greek tragedy written 2000 years ago, but if you are using a translation (and most people would), is that in copyright?

Remember that songs consist of words – the lyrics – as well as music. If you are using an opera whose libretto has been translated into English, is the translation in copyright? Hymns can be problematical as old words or poems are often given new tunes and vice versa.

A book may be out of copyright, but a play or film adapted from it may not be. Works left uncompleted at an author's death may be finished by another person – *The Mystery of Edwin Drood* by Charles Dickens is probably the best-known example.

Still pictures

You need to find out who commissioned the work. Was a photographer paid to do the work or was it done by a freelancer? A photographer working for a company or a newspaper may not own the rights to the pictures she or he took; it will depend on what sort of contract the photographer had.

There are associations, such as the Design and Artists Copyright Society (DACS), usually dealing with fine art or music, that will handle negotiations and payments for its members, but not all designers and artists belong to it. You should check whether the company or broadcaster you are working for has some arrangement with such an organization. This will save considerable time and effort, but you still need to check if the person whose work you want to use is a member.

Moving pictures

Most of the problems here arise not only from copyright clearances but also, especially in feature films and television drama productions, the contracts the performers, directors or writers originally signed. There will often be residual fees to be paid for repeats of television programmes. Post-1960 films may need clearance from actors, writers, the director and (if applicable) stunt men.

Productions made before the advent of home video will not have included these kind of rights in the original contracts and your organization may need to negotiate fees for their use with individuals, especially if you are working on a corporate or training video or one made only for the home video market.

News footage is protected by copyright until 50 years after the end of the year in which it was made.

Feature films are more complicated. The copyright period here now lasts until 70 years after the end of the year in which the last of the following people dies:

1   the principal director of the film
2   the writer of the screenplay who may be different from:
3   the writer of the actual dialogue
4   the composer of music written for and used in the film.

There may be some difficulty in defining who is the 'principal' director or who the 'writer' is, especially where a number of people have worked on the screenplay and script.

The soundtrack of a film may involve two types of copyright – the film soundtrack itself, which is treated as part of the film so the owner of the film copyright will also own this right, and the sound recording copyright, which could be sold to another party to exploit (e.g. by selling recordings of the soundtrack).

You may find that even if a film is out of copyright, the owners of the print charge access fees. You may want to incorporate footage that was shot more than 70 years ago which was included in another programme and which can be obtained through a television company's library rather than the archive containing the original footage. Problems can occur here because whether this can be done or not will depend on the contract agreed when the original production was made. There may have been a clause limiting the number of times it can be shown or even a clause requiring the film to be destroyed after use.

Sound

Music is a complicated area. Composers and songwriters usually sell copyright in their works to music publishers, who thus become the copyright owners. What is then done with the work becomes subject to other agreements.

There are two rights involved in broadcasting music – the right to record (i.e. to record music being played live on to tape or to copy a disc or tape in order to dub it on to a programme) and the right to broadcast music. The first is administered by the Mechanical Copyright Protection Society (MCPS), the second by the Performing Right Society (PRS).

A third organization, Phonographic Performance Ltd (PPL), controls payments made for the use of already recorded music (i.e. commercial discs or tape) which is broadcast, whether this is as part of a music programme on radio or because a commercial record has been dubbed on to a programme. For non-broadcast videos, the equivalent organization is Video Performance Ltd (VPL).

You need to find out if the company for which you are working has any agreements with these organizations and what they are. If there is no agreement, you need to make one. The music business is very litigious and productions are monitored to find out whether broadcasters are complying with the law.

This is easy when you can choose the music being played but on location it may be difficult to avoid music you have no control over (e.g. a football crowd singing, muzak in a hotel lobby or a ghetto-blaster on the shoulder of a passer-by). Ideally, of course, this kind of music would not be in the programme, not because of copyright but because it can create editing problems. If it is unavoidable, however, the rules still apply and if what is being played is commercial music on disc or tape, it must still be cleared. If it is a crowd singing, you need to identify the song.

As a result of the way the music industry is structured worldwide, different companies usually own the rights to a commercial disc in different parts of the world. Thus, clearing a production containing commercial discs for sale around the world is complicated and expensive. Only the film world usually has the resources to do this.

Production music, also called library or mood music, is subject to copyright but can usually be cleared worldwide relatively simply without the complications involved in selling a programme containing commercially recorded music abroad.

Contrary to some belief, sound effects are under copyright and need to be cleared like any other recorded sound. The Mechanical Copyright Protection Society (MCPS) collects royalties on behalf of most, if not all, of the companies making production music and sound effects.

Other factors to be aware of when dealing with music for a production include the following.

- Theme music – the regulations attached to using a piece of music as the theme to a programme or series are different from those applied to music within a production.

- Arrangements – the music you are dealing with may be out of copyright, but the arrangement of it may have been done only recently. If a brass band is playing the overture to *The Marriage of Figaro* (Mozart, d. 1791), you will need to check if the arrangement for brass band as opposed to a full orchestra is in copyright. Folk music is another area where, although the song may be trad or anon, the arrangement may have been done last week and may constitute a copyright element.
- Unfinished works – it is not only Schubert who left symphonies unfinished. Many composers, especially in earlier periods, wrote down only the tune, leaving harmonies and orchestrations unrecorded. Modern editors may have completed a work you wish to use.

The spoken word

Copyright in the spoken word was clarified by the 1988 Act. Since then the spoken word, as in an unscripted interview, has been subject to copyright law. However, only if the contribution is a literary work does this apply. Thus, if you are doorstepping a villain who invites you to 'Naff off', it is unlikely this would be deemed to have any literary merit. However, do not rely on your own definition of what constitutes great literature in a less clear-cut case – talk to an expert.

You can save many problems with people wanting to withdraw an interview they gave you by ensuring that they sign a Release and Consent contract on the spot (you should do this even for vox pops), which gives your organization the rights to their contribution.

Moral rights

This area was created by the 1988 Act, so the law may be different for works created before and after 1 August 1989, the date on which its provisions come into force.

- Paternity is the right to be identified as the author of a work and has to be claimed in writing. When you sit through the credits of a recent film, you usually see the paternity right claimed in some form of words and books now usually have a paragraph detailing who is legally the author. Broadcasters must in general identify the author clearly and prominently. It is worth noting that the paternity right may have been claimed in a way (e.g. a contract) that is not obvious to a researcher, or may have been waived.
- Integrity is the right not to have work subjected to derogatory treatment, i.e. it must not be edited or mucked about with in any way that contravenes the author's intentions. With recorded interviews, there is some overlap with copyright in the spoken word. Get advice.
- Privacy is nothing to do with invasion of privacy. It is the right not to have pictures and videos commissioned for private and domestic use used without permission. The aim is to prevent people selling copies of work they were commissioned to do without the subjects' knowledge.

Burlesques and parodies

If you want to use a parody of a work, you may have to get the original author's permission. Whether you need permission or not depends on how 'substantial' a part of the original work you are using. In the case of a song, of course, the music constitutes a separate copyright element and will have to be cleared in any case.

Major exceptions

- Use of an insubstantial part – using an 'insubstantial' part of a work is as much a question of quality as quantity. The rule-of-thumb is generally, and mistakenly, taken to be 10%, but what is 10% of a four-line poem? You may only show a 30-second clip of a movie, but if it is the pivotal 30 seconds when the villain is unmasked, that would not be regarded as insubstantial.
- Fair dealing – there are various conditions under which a copyright holder's permission does not need to be obtained before using his or her work. In all cases, only enough of the work to make the point can be used – whether the amount used is 'fair' is a matter for experts or the courts to decide.
- Research or private study – this covers copying material, such as extracts from a book or academic article, for the purpose of researching a production.
- Reporting current events – this does not, however, cover photographs.
- Review or criticism of a work – this does not include biographical or general use and where one shades into the other is a matter of expert legal opinion.

Penalties

Sometimes, no matter what research is carried out, it is impossible to clear copyright on every element in a programme. Efforts to find the copyright holder need to be well documented. In general, a copyright holder is entitled only to recover the sum of money that would have been paid if something is used without permission, but to that potential sum must be added the costs of any legal action. The copyright holder may also get an injunction to prevent the production being transmitted or distributed.

Where there is no clear precedent, estimates of the cost of transgressing the law are difficult to make. Any decision whether to do an expensive re-edit or to cross the fingers, transmit and wait for the lawyer's letter needs to be made by someone in authority who will take the responsibility for that decision. Bear in mind, however, that copyright infringement is a criminal offence which can be punished with imprisonment and you will not be popular if you get your employer locked up!

Appendix B: The law and ethics

The laws that are likely to affect people working in the media divide into four broad areas. Note that this section gives details of UK laws. Most countries will have laws covering the same divisions as those given here, but you will need to check.

Many lawyers spend their working lives arguing whether a casual remark is or is not defamatory or whether an action was done maliciously. The ramifications of the law are too complex for people doing research to rely solely on their own knowledge and judgement. It is one thing to know the wording of an Act, but another to know how it has been, or will be, interpreted, thus establishing a precedent in law. Some aspects of the law have not yet been tested in the courts. The further reading list gives books containing much more detail than can be included here. This section gives only an indication of potential problems and a very limited summary of the complex laws that surround these subjects. Seek advice because this, like copyright, is an area where a little learning is a dangerous thing.

Some areas of public life, such as statements in Parliament, in courts and other legal proceedings, such as tribunals, and in government documents are considered privileged. Those making them are protected from legal action, but only in those circumstances. An MP may risk proceedings if she or he repeats outside the House of Commons a statement made inside. The media has only qualified privilege when reporting which means that there must be some public interest and that the report was neither inaccurate nor made maliciously.

Dealing with the government

- Election law – under the Representation of the People Act 1983, legislation applies to the broadcasting and reporting of elections. This period begins, in the case of a General Election, with the announcement of the date Parliament is to be dissolved or the Queen's announcement that she intends to dissolve Parliament. For by-elections, this starts with the issue of the writ. There are also regulations covering elections to the European Parliament.
- Official secrets – the government can classify anything, even down to the menu in a Civil Service canteen, as an official secret, but there are six major categories relating to defence and national security. The Defence Press and Broadcasting Advisory Committee only offers 'guidance', not legal restrictions. DA notices are sent to newspaper editors and television companies but, if you are working for an independent company that does not receive them, they can be obtained easily.
- Sedition – can be defined as 'words which are likely to disturb the internal peace and government of a country'.
- Reporting Parliamentary proceedings – there is some overlap here with the laws on copyright and defamation. Recordings of proceedings can be used mainly for news and current affairs or educational programmes. Clips in light entertainment or magazine programmes must be used with caution and following expert advice.

- Inquiries – although public inquiries are usually held in public, the Secretary of State can direct that evidence considered contrary to the national interest should not be reported.

Reporting legal proceedings

Legal cases divide into the criminal and the civil. Broadly speaking, criminal law covers crimes which damage society generally and civil cases cover actions where an individual has been damaged in some way. In the first situation, the Crown prosecutes. In the second, the individual sues. There are many other semantic distinctions in the way cases are reported; too many to list here. For more information see the further reading list (p. 140).

- Contempt of court and intention to commit contempt of court – these cover anything that might prejudice the outcome of a trial.
- Appeals – someone who was convicted of an offence may later be cleared on appeal and this needs to be checked. Appeals either against the verdict or the length of the sentence sometimes take place a long time after the original trial and may not receive a great deal of publicity so you need to be careful about this.
- Rehabilitation of Offenders Act 1974 – convictions are regarded as spent and, therefore, should not be referred to, after a specified length of time, which varies according to the severity of the sentence, not the crime.
- Juveniles – a child is under 14, a young person is over 14 but under 18. Unless reporting restrictions are lifted by the Court or the Home Secretary, the names or any information (e.g. parents' names or addresses of school) that might identify a juvenile involved in any legal process (including tribunals, custody and wardships cases) may not be disclosed.
- Sexual offences – victims of various sexual offences are granted anonymity but for some offences this applies to females only, for example intercourse with a girl under 13 or one aged between 13 and 16. This restriction can be lifted by a magistrate or a judge and a woman who is raped may also agree to be identified.
- Civil actions – a judge may, or sometimes must, hear some civil actions 'in chambers' (i.e. in private). Reporting what happened there may constitute contempt of court.
- Bankruptcy, company liquidation, tribunals and inquests – are all legal proceedings to which various restrictions apply.

Dealing with individuals

- Defamation, libel and malicious falsehood – the first two are something that judges say, would 'tend to lower the plaintiff in the estimation of a right-thinking member of society' and like many legal definitions, begs more questions than it answers. The third is something that might damage the person named, even if it does not criticize him or her. There are defences – is what was said true and can it be proved, or is it fair comment, not done maliciously, factually based and on a matter of public interest?

- Breach of confidence – this applies to information given in confidence. This might not be directly given to a researcher or journalist by the person to whom it relates. It might come through someone who was told something in confidence or from a person, such as an employee of a company, whose contract of employment has a confidentiality clause, either written or implicit. Some people, such as doctors or priests, have a professional obligation not to repeat things told to them. This is also a potential growth area for those who feel their privacy has been invaded. They may claim that information about them was obtained in circumstances of confidentiality.
- Race relations – under the Public Order Act 1986, care needs to be taken when reporting what someone said if it is likely to stir up hatred against any racial group. Even though it may be made plain that what was said is illegal, the act of repeating it might be illegal. This also applies to defamation – reporting a defamatory statement made by someone else may lead to legal action.

Children

A number of items of legislation cover the use of children in productions. The regulations largely apply to productions where children are giving a performance, but if you are working on a documentary involving children for long periods, you need to ensure that you do not transgress the laws.

There are limits to the hours, including rehearsals, that children may work and they must have a responsible adult, parent or chaperone with them. If they are to be used over a long period, rest periods and educational facilities may have to be provided. They must have their parent's or guardian's permission to appear and may also need permission from their headteacher or local authority. Schoolchildren need to be licensed to perform if they will be working more than 4 days in 6 months. (See the table on p. 102.)

There are other restrictions applying to children. Under 12, they cannot take part in any potentially dangerous performance. Between 12 and 16, they need a licence to be trained for any potentially dangerous activity. A child under 13 cannot drive any farm vehicle, including tractors. Regulatory body standards and codes of practice impose other limits. Children should not, for example, be exposed to any kind of distress which can apply to both a part they might be playing in a drama or questions put to them in a news or documentary programme.

Working with animals

It is not just because of their unpredictable behaviour that people are warned against working with animals. There are four main Acts that apply to use of animals when filming in England – some of the regulations are different in Scotland and Northern Ireland.

- Protection of Animals Act 1911 – this basically legislates against the ill-treatment of animals.
- Performing Animals (Regulation) Act 1925 – under this, people must have a licence, issued by the local authority, to exhibit or train performing animals, as in a circus. The exceptions are the police, military, agricultural

establishments or those doing so for sporting purposes. This may be relevant to a production wanting to use trained animals.

- Cinematograph Films (Animals) Act 1937 – this prevents the showing of any film where cruelty to animals was involved in its making. Under the provisions of this Act, even if you are making a programme about a cruel and illegal practice, such as badger-baiting, you may not be able to record or show what happens.
- Dangerous Wild Animals Act 1976 – this requires anyone keeping a wild animal privately to have a licence. Circuses, zoos, pet shops and certain scientific laboratories are excluded. There is a very long list of species which are, for the purposes of the Act, defined as wild (from aardvarks to wolverines, via cassowaries, okapi and pronghorns). You may also need an encyclopaedia of wildlife to find out if the exotic pet being kept in a block of flats is legally entitled to be there.

Different regulations apply to domestic animals. The Animal Welfare section of the local Department for Environment, Food and Rural Affairs (DEFRA) branch can give advice and, on occasions, will need to know what you are doing with farm animals or wild, endangered and protected species. If you want to bring an animal into the country to film it, Customs and Excise also become involved.

Getting animals to locations can present problems. Moving both pigs and cattle requires special permits. The local Animal Health Office will advise. Restrictions on transporting other animals in parts of the country apply when there are outbreaks of particular virulent diseases, such as foot and mouth disease, swine fever or rabies. Check with the local branch of DEFRA.

The RSPCA has issued guidelines about working with animals. Most are concerned with using animals in drama productions, but there is also good advice about dealing with animals generally. Above all, patience and consideration for the animal's welfare, not just the avoidance of cruelty, are required. A tired, unhappy or unwell animal will not only come across badly but may also be dangerous to performers, contributors and crew. Any injury at all, whether to animals or humans, should be treated immediately, so find out where the local vet and hospital are.

Miscellaneous Acts

As well as the laws relating to the government, legal proceedings and individuals either human or animal, there are five other Acts which need to be taken into account. The first two affect what can be shown; the third, how research information can be stored; and the fourth the access police may have to research material.

- Obscene Publications Act 1959–1999 – the 1999 Act says that 'for purposes of this Act an article shall be deemed obscene if, in whole or in part, it portrays, deals with or relates to any of the activities set out in the Schedule'.
- Police and Criminal Evidence Act 1984 (known as PACE) – this allows the police to obtain journalistic material, including video tapes, to use in evidence where a serious arrestable offence has been committed. A judge must

approve an order and the police must give notice that they are applying for an order before the material is surrendered.

- Data Protection Acts 1984 and 1998 – these require that people must be given access to what information is held on them. Data must be fairly and lawfully processed; processed for limited purposes; adequate, relevant and not excessive; accurate; not kept longer than necessary; processed in accordance with the data subject's rights; secure; and not transferred to other countries without adequate protection. You must be careful about potentially defamatory remarks (e.g. 'alcoholic' or 'pain to work with'). Measures must be taken to prevent unauthorized people gaining access to them and, as far as possible, to prevent accidental loss or destruction of the data. Those who hold information about living people must register their computer with the Data Registration Registrar at the Office of the Information Commissioner, which is now also responsible for Freedom of Information. Paper files may, in some circumstances, fall within the remit of the 1998 Act.

- Human Rights Act 1998 – this is intended to protect individuals against having their rights breached by authorities. Two competing rights – to privacy and freedom of expression – are enshrined in the legislation and present problems to programme-makers and journalists. Cases going through the courts produce and will produce precedents on which researchers must seek expert advice.

- Blasphemy – this can only be against the tenets of Christianity. The Christian churches themselves seem disinclined to pursue productions that might be thought blasphemous but, because it is still a common-law offence, individuals can bring private prosecutions. As Salman Rushdie's experiences show, even if other faiths cannot call in the law to protect them against blasphemy, they can still create trouble for you and your company.

Ethics

What is an ethical consideration in the UK can be legally enforceable elsewhere in the world, so aspects of the law overseas must be taken into account if you are working on a co-production or hoping for overseas sales.

In most situations, the people you deal with need to trust you and this starts with how you represent yourself to them. There is nothing wrong with promoting yourself slightly from researcher to assistant producer or whatever if you are dealing with someone to whom status matters, but you should not directly lie about your production's status. Thus if you have not yet been commissioned by a broadcaster, do not say that you are doing something for Channel 4 or for the BBC. This can be a matter of careful wording – you can say you are gathering material for a programme to be submitted to a company, for example.

None of this applies to investigative reporting, where you may find yourself pretending to be an ordinary punter in order to expose wrongdoing. This area presents a whole can of legal and ethical worms. You need to get advice.

Your next responsibility is to the contributors. Very few people who have not encountered the media realize the impact on their lives of appearing in it. You need to take this into account for them. Could their co-operation lead to criminal prosecution, for example? The production can also get into very tricky legal waters when dealing with criminals. What are their family, friends and neighbours likely to feel and do? How will what they say affect their job prospects, either now or in the future? These have to be balanced against the public good and the right to know, but as a general rule, people should be allowed to make an informed decision about whether or not to participate.

You also need to consider how true a representation of the interviewee the material you gather is. In television, where there is usually time between the initial contact and the recording of an interview, people have time to reconsider their position, but in radio, where most interviews are simply taped on the spot, this is a serious matter. All sorts of outside events can influence what a person says – a difficult journey to work may have put the interviewee in a bad mood, so that what is said is more emphatic and severe than the situation warrants.

There are other ethical considerations relating to contributors. It is a maxim that sources should always be protected. This is not solely a matter of altruism. If you become known as a person who betrays sources, people will be less willing to help you in the future. Although this goes against the grain, you may have to destroy papers and other information received where these might identify who sent them. Although certain types of journalistic material are excluded from the Police and Criminal Evidence Act 1984, the police have powers to obtain an order to take material in defined circumstances. These could reveal sources.

Under the Broadcasting Act 1990, various areas are controlled in broadcast programmes. They are:

- violence
- breaches of good taste and decency
- encouragement or incitement to crime
- anything that might lead to public disorder
- anything offensive to public feeling.

These are not defined in law, but are covered in the broadcasters' codes of practice. There is a 9 pm watershed – material shown after that time can be more powerful on the assumption that children will not be watching. In addition to these, there are a whole host of other areas of sensitivity which need to be considered. The broadcasters have detailed guidelines on, for example, 'bad' language, which is something about which viewers are very exercised.

Programme sponsorship

The Independent Television Commission issues a Code of Programme Sponsorship defining how and in what circumstances programmes or parts of programmes can have production costs met, either in whole or part, by an organization not involved in programme-making in order to promote itself. There are certain companies that cannot sponsor programmes, such as those banned from advertising on television or radio or makers of prescription-only drugs. Political organizations are also forbidden to advertise. PPBs (party political broadcasts) are billed and announced as such. News and current affairs programmes and business programmes may not be sponsored. The BBC also has guidelines covering co-productions and co-funding.

Most of the stipulations, especially those to do with credits, will be dealt with by the producer, but the areas where the researcher needs to be aware of the rules is the content. This is particularly important when the researcher is involved in directing sequences at an event which is being sponsored or support material is being supplied. The sponsor must be clearly identified at the beginning and end of the programme, but any references designed to promote the company's products or activities within it must be editorially justified and not given undue prominence. Be especially careful when tobacco companies are involved because, although they may legitimately be sponsoring an event your programme is covering, advertising tobacco is banned. The sponsor must be identified in support material.

Whether a programme is being sponsored or not, you need to be careful about logos and products that appear within it. Never promise companies credits or on-air publicity. You should also make sure that logos do not appear, unless it is impossible to shoot round them, in which case you must minimize their prominence or even edit them out by pixillation. Keep an eye on what appears in the background of a shot or what people are wearing, such as clothing with logos and slogans that promote their organization.

Law and ethics checklist

Copyright

- What words, pictures and sound are included in the production?
- When did the creator of a work die? Was it more or less than 70 years ago?
- When were any photographs taken? Was it before or after 1st June 1957?
- Are there any moral rights in works created after 1st August 1989?

The Law

- Is the programme dealing with any aspect of government or going out at the time of an election?
- Are any of the contributors, or have they been, involved in any legal proceedings?
- Could anything in the production be construed as obscene, defamatory or blasphemous?
- Are there any race relations issues?
- Could anything revealed in the production be construed as a breach of confidence or human rights?
- Will the production be featuring children?
- Will the production be featuring animals?
- How do the Data Protection Acts affect my record keeping?

Ethics

- Which company or organization's codes of practice apply to my work?
- What are the implications of any sponsorship of the programme, either ethically or legally?
- How could the contributors be affected by their appearance in the production?

Co-productions and overseas sales

- Are there legal/ethical differences in any country where the production is being shown?

Further reading and useful addresses

Working in the media

Books
Chantler, Paul and Harris, Simon (1997). *Local Radio Journalism*. Focal Press.
Langham, Josephine (1997). *Lights, Camera, Action: Working in Film, Television and Video*. British Film Institute.
Llewellyn, Shiona (2000). *A Career Handbook for TV, Radio, Film, Video and Interactive Media*. Skillset.
Selby, Michael (1997). *Careers in Television and Radio*. Kogan Page.

There are a number of books covering communication skills and working as part of a team, which you will find in the local library or bookshop. The following books contain useful information on all aspects of production so will also provide further information for other sections.

Crisp, Mike (1996). *Practical Director*, Second Edition. Focal Press.
Croton, Gordon (1986). *From Script to Screen*. BBC Television Training.
Fraser, Cathie (1990). *The Production Assistant's Survival Guide*. BBC Television Training.
Freeman, Diane (1997). *The Production Handbook*. PACT.
Gates, Richard (1999). *Production Management for Film and Video*, Third Edition. Focal Press.
Keith, Michael C. (1996). *The Radio Station*. Focal Press.
McLeish, Robert (1999). *Radio Production*, Fourth Edition. Focal Press.
Millerson, Gerald (1994). *Effective TV Production*, Third Edition. Focal Press.
Ward, Peter, Bermingham, Alan and Wherry, Chris (2000). *Multiskilling for Television Production*. Focal Press.

Organization
National Training Organization for broadcast, film, video and multi-media provides information on all aspects of training for and working in these media: Skillset, 2nd Floor, 103 Dean Street, London W1D 3TH (tel.: 020-7534 5300).

Developing, research and selling ideas

Books
Buzan, Tony (1994). *Mind Map Book*. E. P. Dutton.
Viljoen, Dorothy (1997). *The Art of the Deal*. PACT. This covers the business aspects of production-making, including sources of finance, production agreements, contracts and rights. Although aimed at those involved in production management, it gives details of the type of information commissioners need and so is useful when developing and selling ideas.

Sources of information and contributors

Books

Most trade associations produce a yearbook or a list of members which you should be able to find in the reference section of a large library. You will also find encyclopaedias, the *Guinness Book of Records*, books of quotations, biographical dictionaries, maps, etc.

Councils, Committees and Boards, including Government Agencies and Authorities. CBD Research.
Directory of British Associations and Associations in Ireland. CBD Research.
Family Welfare Association. *Charities Digest.*
Fisher, Paul and Peak, Steve. *The Media Guide.* Fourth Estate. (Published annually)
Millard, Patricia (ed.). *Trade Associations and Professional Bodies of the United Kingdom.* Gale Research International. (Published annually)
Willings Press Guide. Hollis Directories.

Illustrative material

Books

Ballantyne, James (ed.) (2001). *Researcher's Guide to British Film and Television Collections.* British Universities Film and Video Council.
Ballantyne, James (ed.) (1983–1993). *Researcher's Guide to British Newsreels.* (3 vols.) British Universities Film and Video Council.
Museums Year Book. Museums Association.
Evans, Hilary and Evans, Mary. *The Picture Researcher's Handbook. (6th edn).* Routledge.
Montagu, Ralph (1991). *The Televion Graphics Handbook* plus *CD-ROM (7th edn).* BBC Television Training.
Weerasinghe, Lali (1989). *Directory of Recorded Sound Resources in the UK.* British Library.

Organizations

British Association of Picture Libraries and Agencies (BAPLA), 18 Vine Hill, London EC1R 5DZ (tel.: 020-7731 1780; Website: www.bpla.org.uk).
Federation of Commercial Audio Visual Libraries (FOCAL) International Ltd, Pentax House, South Hill Avenue, South Harrow, Middlesex HA2 0DU (tel.: 020-8423 5853; Website: www.focalint.org.uk), is the UK-based international organization for audio-visual libraries and the professional film researchers who access them. Their members' guide gives a list of all members and what footage, in general terms, the libraries hold and what the researchers have worked on if you need a specialist film researcher.
Moving Image Society, BKSTS, 5 Walpole Court, Ealing Studios, Ealing Green, London W5 5ED (tel.: 020-7242 8400; Website: www.bksts.com) produces a series of wallcharts on film and video formats.

Locations and studios

Books

Jarvis, Peter (1998). *The Essential TV Director's Handbook*. Focal Press.
Small, Robin (2000). *Production Safety for Film, Television and Video*. Focal Press.

Recording the production

Books

Dinsdale, Stephen (1994). *A Quick Crib to Television Stage Management*. BBC Television Training. Although this covers drama production, many of the topics covered are relevant to documentaries and entertainment programmes.
Lyver, Des and Swainson, Graham (1995). *Basics of Video Production*. Focal Press.
Rowlands, Avril (2000). *The Continuity Supervisor*, Fourth Edition, Media Manual Series. Focal Press.

Organization

Radio Communications Agency, New King's Beam House, 22 Upper Ground, London SE1 9SA (tel.: 020 7211 0211; Website: www.radio.gov.uk). It issues licences for walkie-talkies at events.

Editing

Books

Browne, Steve E. (1996). *Video Editing: A Post-Production Primer*, Third Edition. Focal Press.

Writing

Books

The Economist (2001). *Style Guide*. Although intended for print journalism, this book is also valuable in broadcasting. As well as guidance on writing, there is a reference section including such things as capital cities, the names of currencies used in countries and differences between words used in America and Britain, which is useful if you are working on a co-production.
Friedmann, Anthony (2001). *Writing for Visual Media*. Focal Press.
Mansfield, John (1992). *Narration and Editing*. BBC Television Training.

Copyright (Appendix A)

Books

Edwards, Stephen (1997). *Rights Clearances for Film and Television Productions*. PACT.
McCraken, R. and Gilbert, M. (1995). *Buying and Clearing Rights: Print, Broadcast and Multimedia*. British Universities Films and Video Council.

Organizations

Design and Artists Copyright Society Ltd (DACS), Parchment House, 13 Northburgh Street, London EC1V 0AH (tel.: 020-7336 8811; Website: www.dacs.co.uk).

Mechanical Copyright Protection Society (MCPS), Licensing Services, Copyright House, 29–33 Berners Street, London W1T 3AB (tel.: 020-7306 4500 [Media Licensing]; Website: www.mcps.co.uk).

Performing Right Society (PRS), 29–33 Berners Street, London W1P 4AA (tel.: 020-7580 5544; Website: www.mcps-prs-alliance.co.uk).

Phonographic Performance Ltd (PPL), 1 Upper James Street, London SW1F 9DE (tel.: 020-7534 1000; Website: www.ppluk.com).

Video Performances Ltd (VPL) administers rights in music videos for its members. It operates from the same address as PPL.

The law and ethics (Appendix B)

Books

BBC (1993 and updated as necessary). *Guidelines for Factual Programmes*, also at www.bbc.co.uk/info/editorial/prodgl

Crone, Tom, Alberstat, Philip and Cassels, Tom (2001). *Law and the Media*, Fourth Edition. Focal Press.

Greenwood, Walter and Welsh, Tom (2001). *McNae's Essential Law for Journalists*. Butterworths.

Miller, Phil (1998). *Media Law for Producers*, Third Edition. Focal Press.

Organizations

Broadcasting Standards Commission, 7 The Sanctuary, London SW1P 3JS (tel.: 020-7233 0544; Website: www.bsc.org.uk).

Defence Press and Broadcasting Advisory Committee (DPBAC) (The Secretary), Room 704, MoD Metropole Building, London WC2N 5BP (tel.: 020-7218 2206; Website: www.danotice.org.uk).

Independent Television Commission (ITC), 31 Foley Street, London W1P 7LB (tel.: 020-7255 3000; Website: www.itc.org.uk).

The Radio Authority, Holbrook House, Great Queen Street, London WC2B 5DG (tel.: 020-7430 2724; Website: www.radioauthority.org.uk).

Focal Press

www.focalpress.com

Join Focal Press on-line

As a member you will enjoy the following benefits:

- an email bulletin with **information on new books**
- a regular **Focal Press Newsletter**:
  - o featuring a selection of new titles
  - o keeps you informed of **special offers, discounts and freebies**
  - o alerts you to **Focal Press news and events** such as author signings and seminars
- complete access to **free content** and reference material on the focalpress site, such as the focalXtra articles and commentary from our authors
- a **Sneak Preview** of selected titles (sample chapters) *before* they publish
- a chance to have your say on our **discussion boards** and **review books** for other Focal readers

Focal Club Members are invited to give us feedback on our products and services.
Email: worldmarketing@focalpress.com – we want to hear your views!

Membership is **FREE**. To join, visit our website and register. If you require any further information regarding the on-line club please contact:

Emma Hales, Marketing Manager
Email: emma.hales@repp.co.uk
Tel: +44 (0) 1865 314556
Fax: +44 (0)1865 314572
Address: Focal Press, Linacre House,
Jordan Hill, Oxford, UK, OX2 8DP

Catalogue

For information on all Focal Press titles, our full catalogue is available online at www.focalpress.com and all titles can be purchased here via secure online ordering, or contact us for a free printed version:

USA
Email: christine.degon@bhusa.com
Tel: +1 781 904 2607

Europe and rest of world
Email: jo.coleman@repp.co.uk
Tel: +44 (0)1865 314220

Potential authors

If you have an idea for a book, please get in touch:

USA
editors@focalpress.com

Europe and rest of world
focal.press@repp.co.uk

Also available from Focal Press ...

Effective TV Production
Third Edition
Gerald Millerson

Effective TV Production gives a succinct but thorough overview of the production process. Whatever your role in television, this book outlines the main functions of your job, placing them in the context of all other operations and showing how they are interrelated. It describes the essentials of good camerawork and relates them to considerations of audio, staging, lighting, make-up and wardrobe techniques and the way in which a production is developed in approach and style form the initial stages to the moment of shooting.

This edition is substantially revised to reflect developments in technology and contemporary production styles.

**1994 • 224pp • 216 x 138mm • Paperback
ISBN 0 240 51324 X**

Also available from Focal Press ...

TV Technical Operations:
an introduction
Peter Ward

TV Technical Operations is an introduction for new entrants to the broadcast industry and is designed to prepare them for working in mainstream television by discussing essential techniques, technologies and work attitudes.

The author explores: the need to develop a professional approach; the occupational skills needed to meet deadlines, work under pressure and within budget; the need to keep up to date with the technique and technology; the need to maintain a critical appraisal of what and who influences working practices and how these influences affect production and viewers; an introduction to the basic skills needed to work as a multi-skilling technical operator in television; an introduction to broadcast equipment in general production use.

2000 • 240pp • 216 x 138mm • Paperback
ISBN 0 240 51568 4

Also available from Focal Press ...

Audio Techniques for Media Production
Roger Laycock

A comprehensive introductory text, covering all aspects of audio practices in television programme making. It provides a perfect grounding for those starting out in the industry and more advanced material for those keen to build on their prior knowledge of audio in television.

Audio technology has changed dramatically over the last decade and this book deals with all of these changes relating them to current audio techniques in mainstream broadcasting. In offering the core basics as well as more developed skills required it is an ideal vocational guide for those considering a career in broadcasting.

**2002 • 224pp • 216 x 138mm • Paperback
ISBN 0 240 51646 X**

To order your copy phone +44 (0)1865 888180 (UK)
Or +1 800 366 2665 (USA)
Or visit our website on **http://www.focalpress.com**

Also available from Focal Press ...

Grammar of the Shot
Roy Thompson

Grammar of the Shot is a manual for those who are about to embark on a career in shooting pictures. It is aimed at the novice, concentrating purely on the principles of shooting - still the best way to tell a visual story. Written in simple, easy-to-follow language and illustrated with clear uncomplicated line drawings, the book sets down the fundamental knowledge needed to achieve acceptable results.

The book lists, examines and explains the conventions and working practices of taking pictures and is a sister volume to Grammar of the Edit.

1998 • 192pp • 216 x 138mm • Paperback
ISBN 0 240 51398 3

To order your copy phone +44 (0)1865 888180 (UK)
Or +1 800 366 2665 (USA)
Or visit our website on **http://www.focalpress.com**

Also available from Focal Press ...

Grammar of the Edit
Roy Thompson

If you want to get to grips with the editing, either in film or video, this book sets down, in a simple uncomplicated way, the fundamental knowledge you will need to make a good edit between two shots.

Intended primarily for the novice to the craft of editing, Grammar of the Edit is couched in basic, jargon-free, language, illustrated by easy to follow diagrams. It explains in simple terms the fundamental components of an edit, has been extensively class-tested, both in Europe and in developing countries.

1993 • 128pp • 216 x 138mm • Paperback
ISBN 0 240 51340 1

Also available from Focal Press ...

Basic Betacam Camerawork
Third Edition
Peter Ward

Basic Betacam Camerawork offers a complete introduction to both the analogue and digital beta camera formats: Betacam, Digital Beta, Betacam SX and DV & DVCAM. Step-by-step instructions are given covering everything from, pre-recording checklists, to technical camera specifications, instruction on exposure and lighting, composition, editing and sound and techniques for different programme styles.

Aimed at TV camera operators just starting out and film cameramen and women converting to video this book will also appeal to students on film and television production courses

**2001 • 224pp • 216 x 138mm • Paperback
ISBN 0 240 51604 4**

To order your copy phone +44 (0)1865 888180 (UK)
Or +1 800 366 2665 (USA)
Or visit our website on **http://www.focalpress.com**

Also available from Focal Press ...

Digital Video Camerawork
Peter Ward

This manual introduces digital camerawork techniques used in television and video production. Written as a practical guide, the author's step-by-step instructions take you through everything you need to know, from camera controls, to editing, lighting and sound.

This text provides a solid foundation to build upon in the area of digital video production. In a period of transition between analogue and digital acquisition/recording formats Digital Video Camerawork provides up-to-date information familiarizing you with the different production styles and requirements.

Digital Video Camerawork combines clear, technical explanations with practical advice. It is ideal for the less experienced broadcast camera operator and for students on media and television production courses.

**2000 • 240pp • 216 x 138mm • Paperback
ISBN 0 240 51605 2**

Also available from Focal Press ...

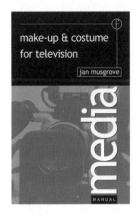

Make-Up and Costume for Television
Jan Musgrove

Offers a step-by step approach for the complete beginner with diagrams to show procedures for a variety of make-up effects, from corrective and character make-up, to period dramas, special effects and prosthetics. It describes the skills required of the job, introduces special make-up products and how to apply them for different effect and sets the context for the make-up artist's role, by considering technical requirements such as lighting, camerawork and chroma-key backgrounds.

It is an ideal introductory guide for students on professional make-up, hairdressing and wardrobe courses, as well as 'front of camera' professionals who require a fuller understanding of the techniques.

2002 • 224pp • 216 x 138mm • Paperback
ISBN 0 240 51660 5